FOOD EDITORS'
HOMETOWN
FAVORITES
COOKBOOK

AMERICAN REGIONAL and LOCAL SPECIALTIES

Edited by
**Barbara Gibbs
Ostmann**
and
Jane Baker

For
The Newspaper Food
Editors and Writers
Association, Inc.

 Dial Publishing
Company

CONTRIBUTING FOOD EDITORS

Bernie Arnold, *Nashville Banner* / Nashville, Tennessee
Jane Baker, *The Phoenix Gazette* / Phoenix, Arizona
Billie Bledsoe, *San Antonio Express-News* / San Antonio, Texas
Pat Baldridge, *Morning Advocate and State-Times* / Baton Rouge, Louisiana
Betsy Balsley, *Los Angeles Times* / Los Angeles, California
Bev Bennett, *Chicago Sun-Times* / Chicago, Illinois
Jane Bennett, *San Francisco Chronicle* / San Francisco, California
Carol Brock, *Daily News* / New York, New York
Marian Burros, *The New York Times* / New York, New York
Ivy Coffey, *The El Reno Daily Tribune* / El Reno, Oklahoma
Elaine Corn, *The Courier-Journal* / Louisville, Kentucky
Kitty Crider, *Austin American-Statesman* / Austin, Texas
Ann Criswell, *Houston Chronicle* / Houston, Texas
Peggy Daum, *The Milwaukee Journal* / Milwaukee, Wisconsin
Sue Dawson, *The Columbus Dispatch* / Columbus, Ohio
Sandra Day, *The Times-Picayune* / *States-Item* / New Orleans, Louisiana
Louise Dodd, *The Courier Herald* / Dublin, Georgia
Barbara Durbin, *The Oregonian* / Portland, Oregon
Sandal English, *Arizona Daily Star* / Tucson, Arizona
Clara Eschmann, *The Macon Telegraph and News* / Macon, Georgia
Janet Beighle French, *The Plain Dealer* / Cleveland, Ohio
Sarah Fritschner, *The Louisville Times* / Louisville, Kentucky
Christine Arpe Gang, *The Commercial Appeal* / Memphis, Tennessee
Ruth Gray, *St. Petersburg Times* / St. Petersburg, Florida
Toni Griffin, *The Tribune* / San Diego, California
Dotty Griffith, *The Dallas Morning News* / Dallas, Texas
Carol Haddix, *Chicago Tribune* / Chicago, Illinois
Marge Hanley, *Indianapolis News* / Indianapolis, Indiana
Phyllis Hanes, *The Christian Science Monitor* / Boston, Massachusetts
Carol Hanson, *The Post-Crescent* / Appleton, Wisconsin
Charlotte Hansen, *The Jamestown Sun* / Jamestown, North Dakota
Ginger Johnston, *The Oregonian* / Portland, Oregon
Pat Hanna Kuehl, *Rocky Mountain News* / Denver, Colorado
Jann Malone, *Richmond Times-Dispatch* / Richmond, Virginia

Karen Marshall, *St. Louis Globe-Democrat* / St. Louis, Missouri
Marilynn Marter, *The Philadelphia Inquirer* / Philadelphia, Pennsylvania
Ann McDuffie, *The Tampa Tribune* / Tampa, Florida
Jane Mengenhauser, *The Journal Newspapers* / Springfield, Virginia
Woodene Merriman, *Pittsburgh Post-Gazette* / Pittsburgh, Pennsylvania
Jane Moulton, *The Plain Dealer* / Cleveland, Ohio
Bernie O'Brien, *Hollywood Sun-Tattler* / Hollywood, Florida
Janice Okun, *Buffalo News* / Buffalo, New York
Barbara Gibbs Ostmann, *St. Louis Post Dispatch* / St. Louis, Missouri
Eleanor Ostman, *St. Paul Pioneer Press and Dispatch* / St. Paul, Minnesota
Nancy Pappas, *The Louisville Times* / Louisville, Kentucky
Anne Byrn Phillips, *The Atlanta Journal-Constitution* / Atlanta, Georgia
Mary Frances Phillips, *San Jose Mercury News* / San Jose, California
Gail Perrin, *The Boston Globe* / Boston, Massachusetts
Mary Alice Powell, *The Blade* / Toledo, Ohio
Helen Wilber Richardson, *The Providence Journal-Bulletin* /
    Providence, Rhode Island
Joyce Rosencrans, *The Cincinnati Post* / Cincinnati, Ohio
Marilyn McDevitt Rubin, *The Pittsburgh Press* / Pittsburgh
Donna Segal, *The Indianapolis Star* / Indianapolis, Indiana
Kit Snedaker, *Los Angeles Herald Examiner* / Los Angeles, California
Dorothy Sorenson, *The Sacramento Bee* / Sacramento, California
Beth Tartan, *Winston-Salem Journal* / Winston-Salem, North Carolina
Jean Thwaite, *The Atlanta Journal-Constitution* / Atlanta, Georgia
Charlyne Varkonyi, *Fort Lauderdale News & Sun Sentinel* /
    Fort Lauderdale, Florida
Evelyn Wavpotich, *The Island Packet* / Hilton Head Island, South Carolina
Diane Wiggins, *St. Louis Globe-Democrat* / St. Louis, Missouri
Fran H. Zupan, *The Columbia Record* / Columbia, South Carolina

Contents

Library of Congress Cataloging in Publication Data

Main entry under title:

Food editors' hometown favorites cookbook.

    Includes index.

    1. Cookery, American.   I. Ostmann, Barbara Gibbs.
II. Baker, Jane.   III. Newspaper Food Editors and
Writers Association (U.S.)

TX715.F673   1984   641.5973   84-10930

ISBN 0-8437-3398-5 (pbk.)

INTRODUCTION

When putting together the recipes for our first cookbook, "Food Editors' Favorites," a collection of tried-and-true personal recipes, we realized we had a double set of treasures. In addition to the family favorites, we discovered a collection of regional and local specialty foods from across the land.

In the beginning, we dubbed these specialties regional junk food. Somehow, junk food didn't seem to be an appropriate category for food editors. Besides, these foods aren't junk. Many of them are fun, frivolous, amusing; others are basic, hearty fare. But what makes them special is that each is unique to its own region, often to its own city or county. These are truly hometown favorites, in the sense that many of them are so localized that they probably have never been heard of outside their own small community.

Have you ever had Chicken Booyah from Wisconsin? Or Toasted Ravioli from St. Louis? Benedictine from Louisville or Devonshire Sandwiches from Pittsburgh? The list goes on and on, making for enjoyable reading and even more enjoyable eating.

We've also included some of the better known regional specialties, such as Chicken-Fried Steak from Texas and Hangtown Fry from California, because the book didn't seem complete without them. But most of the recipes in this book will be foods new to you, providing a mouth-watering look into the culinary melting pot of American foods. In some cases, ingredients may only be available locally. But the recipe will at least provide food for thought.

We'd like to make it clear that these are recipes indigenous to our areas; we make no claim that they are original. When possible, we've given credit where credit is due. But in many cases, the recipes simply evolved and it is difficult, if not impossible, to say from where they came.

A collection as varied as this was made possible only through the network of food editors represented by the Newspaper Food Editors and Writers Association, Inc. (NFEWA). This professional organization was founded in 1974 to encourage communication among food editors and writers, to foster professional ethical standards, to share knowledge about foods and to promote a greater understanding among other journalists.

Although we relied on fellow food editors for recipes for this book, we would be happy to hear from readers about any local specialty foods we might have missed. Perhaps they can be included in a revision of this book, or maybe even a second volume. If you have a hometown favorite you'd like to tell us about, please write: NFEWA Cookbook, c/o Barbara Gibbs Ostmann, 520 East Main Street, Union, Mo. 63084.

We hope you will enjoy exploring the culinary idio-syncracies of this country's cities and towns. It's a tasty experience.

Barbara Gibbs Ostmann
President, NFEWA
1982-1984

Jane Baker
President, NFEWA
1984-1986

Appetizers

Nancy Pappas

The Louisville Times / Louisville, Kentucky

This recipe was originally from Miss Jennie Benedict, who ran a wonderful tea room in Louisville from 1900 until her death in 1928. She also catered posh parties. Eventually the recipe proved so popular it became available ready-made. Some restaurants now offer an "aberrant version"—cream cheese colored green.

BENEDICTINE

12 servings

1 medium cucumber, peeled,
   seeded and grated
2 packages (3 ounces each)
   cream cheese, softened
1 medium onion, grated
½ teaspoon salt

Dash hot pepper sauce
Enough mayonnaise to make
   of spreading consistency
2 drops green food coloring
Bread or crackers

Wring out grated cucumber pulp in clean cloth until quite dry.

Blend cream cheese, cucumber, onion, salt, hot pepper sauce, mayonnaise and food coloring thoroughly in a medium mixing bowl. Serve chilled on buttered white bread cut-outs, or toasted whole wheat or sprouted wheat bread, or with crackers.

Bernie O'Brien

Hollywood Sun-Tattler / Hollywood, Florida

Jane Fisher, widow of Carl Fisher, founder of Miami Beach, always served her famous onion sandwiches as hors d'oeuvres at her own cocktail parties. Mrs. Fisher said, "It takes three days to make them, but they're worth the work. They taste just like you're biting into an apple."

ONION SANDWICHES

Use flat white onions. Soak them in ice cubes in refrigerator overnight. Slice them the next day and soak slices in ice cubes overnight.

On the third day, cut soft, white sandwich bread into rounds using a small cookie cutter. Spread each round with mayonnaise. Drain onion slices and pat dry. Put slices between bread rounds. Wrap in waxed paper and refrigerate for 5 hours. Serve chilled.

The Franciscan Padres brought almonds to California in the middle 1700s. It was found that ideal conditions for growing almonds prevailed in the great central valleys of Sacramento and San Joaquin. Today California is the only place in North America where almonds are grown commercially, and more than half the world's supply of these nuts is now produced here.

Sacramento is the home of the world's largest almond processing plant, hosting many tourist visitors each year. The many flavors of cocktail almonds, which can be tasted during the tour, are the inspiration for many holiday gifts.

FRENCH FRIED ALMONDS

2 cups

Vegetable oil
2 cups blanched whole almonds (see note)
Salt or seasoned salt

Heat oil in a deep-fryer to 360°F. Fry dry blanched almonds in oil until lightly browned, using a deep-fry basket or strainer for easy handling. Drain almonds on absorbent paper and sprinkle with salt while hot.

Note: To prepare blanched almonds, pour boiling water over shelled almonds and let stand just until brown skins can be easily slipped off (2 to 5 minutes). Allow nuts to dry thoroughly before using.

SMOKY COCKTAIL ALMONDS

1 cup

½ teaspoon liquid smoke
2 teaspoons water
1 cup natural (unblanched)
    almonds

1 teaspoon vegetable oil
Salt

Mix liquid smoke and water. Add almonds and toss to coat. Place in a shallow pan; cover and let stand overnight.

Add oil to almonds; toss almonds to coat. Roast in a 300°F oven about 25 minutes, stirring frequently. Sprinkle with salt while hot.

HUNGARIAN ALMONDS

2 cups

1½ tablespoons paprika
1 tablespoon all-purpose
   flour

2 teaspoons garlic salt
1 egg white
2 cups whole natural almonds

Combine paprika, flour and garlic salt in a small bowl; set aside.

Beat egg white until frothy. Add almonds; toss to coat. Drain on paper towels.

Toss almonds with paprika mixture to coat. Spread in a single layer in a greased shallow baking pan. Bake in a 300°F oven 15 to 20 minutes.

Kitty Crider

Austin American-Statesman / Austin, Texas

Whenever Texans want to jazz up a recipe, they add a can of tomatoes with green chilies. Pots of chili, casseroles, dips—every dish knows the zip that can come from this little ten-ounce can.

There are now other brands of tomatoes with green chilies on the market, but Texans have remained loyal to Ro-Tel, a home-state product that has distribution in half a dozen other states. (Incidentally, Ro-Tel tomatoes first came to fame during Lyndon B. Johnson's term as president. His now-famous Pedernales River Chili called for the product. From that time on, it received national recognition, which is quite an accomplishment for a hot little tomato from the small town of Elsa.)

Today the best-known use for these tomatoes is Cheese Dip, or Chile Con Queso, an embarrassingly simple two-ingredient operation that is standard fare for parties, ballgame watching and office occasions.

TEXAS CHEESE DIP

3 cups

1 pound pasteurized American cheese
1 can (10 ounces) tomatoes with green chilies, undrained
   Corn chips

Melt cheese in top of a double boiler, or in a microwave oven or slow cooker. Stir in undrained tomatoes and chilies; blend well, breaking up tomatoes. (For a thicker dip, add more cheese.) Serve warm with corn chips.

Note: Two variations are very popular. (1) Increase cheese to 2 pounds and add 1 pound cooked, crumbled pork sausage. (2) Add 1 pound cooked, crumbled pork sausage and 1 pound browned ground beef.

St. Louisans may take Toasted Ravioli for granted, but it is actually a strictly St. Louis phenomenon. Out-of-towners have never heard of Toasted Ravioli. There are several versions of the origin of the dish. Here's one from local newspaper files.

Mickey Garagiola, of Ruggeri's on the Hill (Italian community) in St. Louis, claims to have been present the night Toasted Ravioli was born. The event wasn't at Ruggeri's, but down the street at a long-gone restaurant called Oldani's, which was one of four Italian restaurants on the Hill in the late 1930s. Louie Oldani employed a German cook named Fritz who was, according to the story, "feeling a bit under the weather" and accidentally dropped a boiled ravioli into hot grease. When the dumpling came to the top, he dropped in a few more, then sent a plateful to the bar. The customers loved them and asked for another order. The Toasted Ravioli was born.

That first Toasted Ravioli was a distant cousin of today's beloved dish. It wasn't breaded or served with meat sauce. Oldani served them at the bar like potato chips or pretzels, according to Garagiola.

This up-to-date version of Toasted Ravioli comes from the Pasta House Company.

TOASTED RAVIOLI

Frozen ravioli, homemade or
  store-bought
Milk
Dry bread crumbs

Vegetable oil for deep-frying
Grated Parmesan cheese
Meat sauce, tomato sauce or
  butter sauce, for dipping

Remove ravioli from freezer. Do not brush off flour that was sprinkled over them before freezing. Pour milk in a small dish. Place bread crumbs in a small dish. Heat oil in a deep-fat fryer or pot to 375°F.

Dip frozen ravioli in milk. Then dip ravioli in bread crumbs. Deep-fry ravioli in hot oil until done, about 3 to 4 minutes, or until golden brown. The squares will sink at first, then rise to top of oil when done. Turn squares as they fry to promote even cooking. Remove from oil; drain well. Sprinkle at once with Parmesan cheese. Serve as is, or with a tomato sauce, meat sauce or butter sauce.

Note: Canned, brine-packed ravioli, well drained, can be used.

Chicken wings are one of the foods for which Buffalo is famous. They are served in all bars and corner taverns, as well as in "fancy" restaurants and pizza joints.

Naturally, no restaurateur is about to divulge his recipe, so we set out to make our own—spying and tasting like mad. After many, many tries, we came up with a recipe with fourteen different ingredients. It was not bad and we printed it. The recipe was a fair success.

About two years later, a reader sent in the recipe that appears here with only two sauce ingredients: Louisiana hot sauce and butter. What do you know? An exact duplicate of restaurant chicken wings. Simplicity and perfection combined!

Incidentally, in Buffalo, chicken wings are always served with celery sticks and Blue Cheese Dressing. No one knows why, but it is part of the ritual. Use the dressing recipe given, or a commercial blue cheese dressing.

BUFFALO CHICKEN WINGS

4 to 6 servings

About 20 to 25 chicken
    wings
Vegetable oil for deep-frying
¼ cup butter or margarine
½ to 1 bottle (2½ ounces)
    Louisiana hot sauce, or to
    taste

Celery sticks
Blue Cheese Dressing (recipe
    follows)

Cut wings in half. Remove wing tips. Deep-fry wings, about half at a time, in hot oil until they are crisp and golden brown, about 10 minutes. (Do not use any batter or crumbs.) Drain wings well.

Melt butter in a saucepan. Add about ½ of the bottle of hot sauce; stir until well blended. (Using ½ bottle will give medium-hot chicken wings. If you like your wings hotter, add the whole bottle, or to taste. If you want them milder, add more butter.)

Place chicken wings in a large container with a cover. Pour sauce over wings; mix well. Serve warm, with celery sticks and Blue Cheese Dressing. Dip the wings and celery sticks in dressing as you eat. Provide plenty of napkins.

BLUE CHEESE DRESSING

2½ cups

2 tablespoons chopped onion
1 clove garlic, minced
¼ cup chopped fresh parsley
1 cup mayonnaise or salad
  dressing
½ cup dairy sour cream

1 tablespoon lemon juice
1 tablespoon white vinegar
¼ cup crumbled blue cheese
Salt, pepper and cayenne, to
  taste

Combine onion, garlic, parsley, mayonnaise, sour cream, lemon juice, vinegar and blue cheese in a medium mixing bowl. Season to taste with salt, pepper and cayenne. Chill for an hour or longer.

Serve as an accompaniment to Buffalo Chicken Wings.

Ruth Gray
St. Petersburg Times / St. Petersburg, Florida

Smoked fish, especially mullet and mackerel, are specialties of the Florida Gulf Coast. You can smoke your own fish or buy it. In my area, consumers can purchase smoked fish in restaurants to take home.

SMOKED FISH DIP

2 cups

¾ pound smoked mullet,
  mackerel or other fish
1 package (8 ounces) cream
  cheese, softened

2 tablespoons half-and-half or
  light cream
2 tablespoons lemon juice
¼ teaspoon garlic salt

Remove any skin or bones from fish. Chop fish fine to make about 1½ cups. Combine fish with cream cheese, half-and-half, lemon juice and garlic salt in a medium mixing bowl; mix well. Chill and serve with crackers or chips.

Note: This dip can be made with fish that is not smoked. Just add ½ teaspoon liquid smoke to cooked, flaked fish with the other ingredients.

Dorothy Sorenson
The Sacramento Bee / Sacramento, California

When the subject of crayfish, or crawdads, comes up, most people think of New Orleans, where they are a popular menu item. However, the Sacramento-San Joaquin Delta region in California produces some 556,000 pounds of crayfish each year, many of which are exported to Sweden, where they are a prized delicacy.

Many Sacramento area fishermen set out crayfish traps and invite their friends to crayfish feeds. Restaurants along the river serve them for appetizers, lunches or for main dishes for dinner.

This simple method is the most popular way to cook them.

CRAYFISH
2 servings

Boiling water
Celery leaves and
   trimmings
2 tablespoons mixed
   pickling spices
1 can (12 ounces) beer

1 lemon, sliced
3 dozen crayfish
Curried Mayonnaise
   (recipe follows),
   or seafood cocktail sauce

Bring water to a boil in a deep kettle. Add celery, spices, beer and lemon. When mixture is boiling briskly, add crayfish and cook 4 to 5 minutes. When they turn red or float to the top, they are done.

Most of the meat is in the tail, but the head contains fat, which is delicious. Crack and eat crayfish with the fingers, dipping meat into Curried Mayonnaise or seafood cocktail sauce.

CURRIED MAYONNAISE
1 cup

1 egg
1 tablespoon red wine vinegar
½ teaspoon salt
½ teaspoon curry powder

½ teaspoon spicy mustard
Freshly ground pepper
1 cup vegetable oil

Place egg, vinegar, salt, curry powder, mustard and pepper in container of a food processor or electric blender. Process until blended. Slowly add oil, a few drops at a time, then faster until mixture is thick and smooth.

Sarah Fritschner

The Louisville Times / Louisville, Kentucky

Louisville is the home of many specialties, including the rolled oyster. This distinctive culinary invention resembles a croquette but is actually three or four oysters dipped in batter, rolled in white cornmeal and then deep-fried. Rolled oysters are eaten with the fingers at picnics, are served as "nibbles" at Louisville bars, or can be the main dish for a light supper.

As with most special dishes, the origin is a source of controversy. Al Kolb, an old-time restaurateur, insisted that his mother brought the recipe from New Orleans. Chefs at Mazzoni's restaurant tell a different story. According to them, back in the 1870s a Frenchman who ran a tavern on Third Street had some oysters left over. For lack of something better to do with them, he whipped up a flour-and-water batter and mixed the oysters in it. Because the oysters were so small, three or four were rolled together in cornmeal to make one great big croquette. Rolled oysters are still prepared this way at Mazzoni's.

This version is from Marion Flexner, a Louisville cookbook author.

LOUISVILLE ROLLED OYSTERS
6 servings

½ cup all-purpose flour	18 medium oysters, drained
1 teaspoon baking powder	1 cup white cornmeal or
¼ teaspoon salt	cracker meal
1 egg, well beaten	Lard or solid shortening,
¼ cup milk, or more as	for deep-frying
needed	Dips of choice

Sift flour, baking powder and salt in a medium mixing bowl. Beat together egg and milk; add to flour mixture and mix well. Batter should be stiff, but if it is too stiff to coat the oysters, add additional milk. Beat until smooth. Put oysters in batter and stir to coat oysters well. Scoop up three oysters at a time and form them by hand into a croquette. Quickly roll croquette in cornmeal, covering it completely. Repeat with remaining oysters. After all croquettes have been formed, dip each again in batter and dust again with cornmeal. At this point, oysters can be refrigerated until time to fry them.

Heat lard to 375°F in a deep-fryer. Put 3 rolled oysters at a time in basket and lower into hot fat. The rolled oysters should cook on all sides; it may be necessary to turn them with a pancake turner. Cook through, about 3 to 4 minutes total cooking time. Drain on paper towels.

Serve rolled oysters hot, with a dipping sauce of choice. The most common choices are ketchup or tartar sauce.

On those long, hot summer days in the office, when bodies and spirits are about to wilt, everyone knows it's time for the house special big chill. Made the slow, old-fashioned way, it's an All-American favorite that knows no regional bounds. For an extra special treat, we like to spice it up.

LEMONADE 1½ *quarts*

6½ **cups water**
⅔ **cup sugar**
3 **lemons**

Make a syrup by placing the sugar and 1⅔ cups water in a saucepan and cook over medium heat, stirring continuously until the sugar dissolves. Dip a pastry brush in hot water and use it to wipe down any sugar crystals sticking to the sides of the pan. Raise the heat, bring the syrup to a boil without stirring, and boil it for one minute before removing the pan from the heat. Peel the lemons, finely chop the peels, and strain the juice. In a separate container stir the lemon peel into the remaining water and add the lemon juice. Add the sugar syrup, mix well, and let stand at room temperature for 3½ hours. Strain the liquid through a colander lined with cheese cloth and refrigerate it several hours until well chilled.

LEMONADE SPICE 1½ *quarts*

5-inch **cinnamon stick**   1 **quart chilled lemonade**
5 **whole cloves**   **ice cubes**
1 **tsp. ground allspice**   **lemon slices, studded with**
2 **cups water**   **whole cloves**
                                    nutmeg to taste

Combine the cinnamon, cloves and allspice with the water in a saucepan. Bring to a boil, reduce the heat, and simmer uncovered for 8 minutes. Strain and chill the liquid. Add the spiced liquid to the chilled lemonade. To serve, pour the spiced lemonade into tall glasses partly filled with ice cubes. Garnish each drink with a lemon slice and a sprinkling of nutmeg.

Soups, Stews and Salads

Phyllis Hanes

The Christian Science Monitor / Boston, Massachusetts

The word chowder comes from the French "la chaudière," a huge copper pot in which French fishermen would share the catch at the return of the fleet. The tradition came to Canada with the French and then moved into New England, where the word became chowder.

The most famous chowders of this area today are the fish and clam chowders, with salt pork as essential an ingredient as the fish itself.

New Yorkers and people from Connecticut and Rhode Island add tomatoes to their fish chowder, and it is a fine dish, but this is never done in northern New England. Down Easters can become so annoyed at the idea of tomatoes in a clam or fish chowder that the Maine legislature once introduced a bill to outlaw forever the mixing of clams and tomatoes.

Since my father and both grandfathers were Down East fishermen, I consider our family recipe to be as authentic as you can get. According to some very old books describing chowders, herbs were sometimes added. However, in my family, no herbs, parsley or paprika are used.

MAINE FISH CHOWDER   *6 to 8 servings*

1 2-inch cube salt pork	3½ to 4 pounds haddock or
1 medium onion, chopped	cod, with bone
4 cups cubed or sliced	Water
potatoes	1 quart milk
1 tablespoon salt	Pepper, to taste

Cut salt pork into tiny cubes and cook in a large pot until light golden; remove with a slotted spoon and set aside.

Discard all but about 1 tablespoon of the fat. Add onion and cook over low to medium heat until soft.

Add potatoes and salt to the kettle. Place fish on top of potatoes, and add enough water to cover potatoes and steam fish. Bring to a boil and reduce heat to simmer for 10 to 15 minutes until both fish and potatoes are done. (Remove bone from fish, which can be done easily after fish has cooked.) When fish flakes easily into large pieces and potatoes are done, add milk and correct seasonings. Top with pork cubes. Serve with pickles and common or pilot crackers.

Note: Some New Englanders use half-and-half or half milk and half evaporated milk. Some add a tablespoon of butter before serving. Although some people use bacon instead of salt pork or use herbs or parsley, it is not typical.

There are many versions of clam chowder. The main thing is that a TRUE New England clam chowder has no flour—just fried salt pork, milk, clams, salt, pepper and butter.

The following recipe does use some flour, and even allows for the addition of thyme, if desired. Although it may not be the most authentic version, it is perhaps the most realistic for today's tastes and ingredients. It is adapted from a recipe in our newspaper cookbook written by Margaret Deeds Murphy.

NEW ENGLAND CLAM CHOWDER   *1 quart*

4 tablespoons diced salt pork
  (see note)
1 medium onion, chopped
1 to 2 tablespoons all-purpose
  flour
2 cups strained clam juice
1 medium potato, peeled and
  diced

Pinch dried thyme (optional)
1 cup milk
1 cup chopped clams (see note)
Salt and freshly ground
  pepper, to taste
Butter
Pilot crackers

Slowly cook salt pork in a 1½-quart saucepan until pieces are crisp. Remove salt pork and reserve.

Add onion to drippings in saucepan and cook, stirring, until tender but not browned. Stir in flour, then add clam juice. Add potato and thyme. Bring to a boil, cover and simmer 15 minutes, or until potatoes are tender. Stir in milk and reheat, but do not let boil. Add clams and reheat, but do not let boil. Taste; add salt and pepper as needed.

Ladle clam chowder into bowls, top each with a pat of butter and sprinkle with reserved salt pork pieces. Serve with pilot crackers.

Note: Salt pork is the traditional ingredient for clam chowder, but many cooks today prefer bacon because it is more convenient. Substitute 4 slices bacon, diced, for salt pork, if desired. Leave bacon in saucepan and cook with other ingredients instead of sprinkling on top as for salt pork.

If you use fresh clams, strain juice through cheesecloth to remove sand and bits of shells. Wash clams well and chop in an electric blender or food processor.

Minnesota, the country's leading producer of both truly "wild" and paddy-grown wild rice, also produces a banquet of recipes for the native grain. This soup recipe, borrowed from a Twin Cities hotel, has become a staple starter for company and holiday meals at our house.

MINNESOTA WILD RICE SOUP

12 *servings*

½ cup uncooked wild rice
1 large onion, diced
2 large fresh mushrooms, diced, or 1 can (4 ounces) sliced
    mushrooms, drained
½ cup butter
1 cup all-purpose flour
8 cups hot chicken broth
    Salt and pepper, to taste
1 cup half-and-half or light cream
2 tablespoons sherry or dry white wine

Add wild rice to 2 cups water in saucepan. Simmer for 45 minutes. Set aside.

Sauté onion and mushrooms in butter in a large pan about 3 minutes, or just until vegetables soften. Stir in flour, cooking and stirring until flour is mixed in, but do not let it begin to brown. Slowly add hot chicken broth, stirring until all of vegetable-flour mixture is well blended. Stir in cooked rice. Season with salt and pepper. Heat thoroughly. Stir in half-and-half. Add sherry and heat gently, but do not boil.

Note: Soup can be prepared to the point of adding half-and-half, set aside until needed, then reheated adding half-and-half and sherry.

Bev Bennett

Chicago Sun-Times / Chicago, Illinois

Every city has some fishy stories buried somewhere in its past. It's an essential part of a city's character. For example, in San Francisco, cioppino—a heady, herbed fish soup—is a readily identifiable element of the city's cuisine.

A city needs a fish soup to call its own, so I recently set out to compose one for Chicago, scaling all recipe possibilities. First, an assessment of what this culinary ode should be.

Chicago is a bold, gutsy city, and the soup should reflect that. No delicate cream base for Chicago. This is a city of tomatoes, onions and garlic. Chicago is also spicy, sometimes sweet, but with a bite.

It should salute our ethnic mix: Italians, Latinos, Irish, Polish and

Germans. It should include the natural bounty of the Midwest—corn, potatoes, tomatoes and grains. And, lest I forget, it should include the local catch.

I briefly considered alewives, but noticed that not even the seagulls would eat them. Not a fitting start for our city's fish soup. However, Lake Michigan does supply a wealth of Coho salmon and smelt. Smelt fishing is in fact an institution. It probably draws as many people to the lakefront as the bikini-filled Oak Street beach will on a good summer Sunday.

Then for added good measure, I included whitefish, available fresh in many supermarkets. While not immediately local, coming from Lake Superior waters, it's certainly a species Chicagoans are familiar with and enthused about.

Putting all those essentials together—onions, garlic, green pepper, celery and tomatoes with Irish potatoes, a can of Stroh's beer, Italian oregano, Mexican chili peppers, Illinois corn, Lake Michigan salmon and smelt and Lake Superior whitefish, I've created what I'd call a fine kettle of fish for Chicago.

CHICAGO FISH SOUP
4 main-course servings

1 medium onion, chopped
2 cloves garlic, finely minced
½ cup chopped green pepper
1 cup thinly sliced celery
3 tablespoons butter
1 can (29 ounces) tomatoes, coarsely chopped
1 cup diced potato
1 can or bottle (12 ounces) beer
1 teaspoon dried crushed basil
1 teaspoon dried crushed oregano
1 teaspoon salt
   Dash pepper
¼ teaspoon crushed dried red peppers
1 cup fresh corn kernels
½ pound salmon steaks, boned, flesh cut into cubes
¼ pound whitefish, cubed (or use ½ pound whitefish and omit
   smelt)
¼ pound smelt, boned and cubed

Sauté onion, garlic, green pepper and celery in butter in a large saucepot or Dutch oven until tender, about 15 minutes. Add tomatoes, potatoes and beer. Add basil, oregano, salt, pepper and red peppers. Simmer until potatoes are almost tender, about 15 minutes. Add corn and fish. Continue simmering about 10 minutes, or until fish is done.

Charlyne Varkonyi

Fort Lauderdale News & Sun Sentinel / Fort Lauderdale, Florida

Just as Pennsylvanians go to New York City for the weekend, we go to the Bahamas. When we can't get there, we hunger for a taste of island food.

Some of the most authentic island cooking is produced at the Bimini Sea Shack on State Road 84 in Fort Lauderdale. It's one of those places that you would never think of trying. It's in a rundown section where bikers on Harleys are part of the ambiance. Culinary clues are slim once you go inside. The tables and booths have no tablecloths, napkins are paper and the menu is written on a chalkboard, which is brought to your table and plopped on a chair.

Ironically, most diners don't drive here; they cruise in on their boats. Owner Hazel Day says many of the boat people take her food on trips. One couple ordered a quart of Conch Chowder and four loaves of Bimini Bread (see page 111) for their trip to Bimini in the Bahamas.

CONCH CHOWDER
3 quarts

½ pound bacon, finely chopped
1 large onion, chopped
2 cans (28 ounces each) tomatoes, cut up
1 can (46 ounces) tomato juice
3 cans (12 ounces each) whole kernel corn
5 pounds potatoes, peeled and diced
2 pounds conch (a type of seafood available in Florida and in good
     fish markets elsewhere)
2 cups cold water
1 teaspoon salt, or to taste
½ teaspoon pepper
½ teaspoon hot pepper sauce, or more, to taste

Fry bacon in a skillet. Add onion and cook until onion is tender. Remove bacon and onion from skillet with a slotted spoon and put in a 6-quart kettle. Add tomatoes with liquid, tomato juice, corn with liquid and potatoes. Cover and cook until potatoes are almost done, about 20 minutes.

Meanwhile, prepare conch. Slice into thin slices and pound on each side with a meat mallet or the back of a heavy spoon to help tenderize it. Then cut into small pieces.

Pour cold water into vegetable mixture to stop it from boiling. Add conch. Cook slowly at a simmer until conch is tender, about 25 minutes. Do not boil. Season with salt, pepper and hot pepper sauce.

Ann McDuffie
The Tampa Tribune / Tampa, Florida

An easy do-ahead dinner might feature Picadillo, sort of a Spanish or Cuban beef stew. Picadillo is good with a big green salad and a hearty red wine. Crusty bread, too, of course.

PICADILLO   *6 servings*

2 pounds ground beef (chuck or rump)
  Olive oil
1 medium onion, chopped
½ medium green pepper, chopped
1 large ripe tomato, peeled, seeded and chopped, or
    2 to 3 tomatoes if preferred
1 clove garlic, minced
1 bay leaf
½ teaspoon dried crushed oregano
1 bottle (3 ounces) capers, drained (optional)
8 pimiento-stuffed green olives, sliced into rounds
1 tablespoon red wine vinegar
3 to 4 tablespoons tomato sauce
¼ cup Burgundy wine
2 to 3 drops hot pepper sauce
  Handful of raisins
  Dash ground nutmeg
½ cup water if needed
  Salt to taste
½ teaspoon light brown sugar if needed

Brown ground beef in a spoonful of olive oil in a large skillet or Dutch oven until red disappears. Add onion, green pepper, tomato, garlic, bay leaf, oregano and capers. Stir and cook, covered, about 30 minutes.

Add olives, vinegar, tomato sauce, wine, hot pepper sauce, raisins and nutmeg. Stir well. Cook, uncovered, about 5 minutes.

Add water, salt and brown sugar, if needed. (Dish is not supposed to be sweet.) Cover and cook over low heat about 30 minutes, until most of liquid is absorbed.

Serve over long-grain white rice with ripe, fried plaintains, if available.

Note: It is easy to multiply Picadillo for a crowd. Or, if more people show up than you expect, you can easily stretch this dish as the Cubans do by stirring in a couple of potatoes, cubed and fried in oil.

The capers can be omitted, if desired, but I like them. Some of my Cuban friends also stir in a handful of walnut halves.

Jane Benet

San Francisco Chronicle / San Francisco, California

Cioppino is a San Francisco favorite. It is a fish stew of sorts and, as with the bouillabaisse of southern France, it relies pretty much on whatever fresh fish and shellfish are available. Serve it with plenty of hot, buttered French bread, glasses of a good dry white wine and a tossed green salad, if desired. It's messy to eat, so be sure to provide plenty of napkins.

CIOPPINO
6 to 10 servings

1 cup fine olive oil
2 large onions
1 large bunch parsley, stems removed
2 large or 3 medium cloves garlic
2 cans (29 ounces each) solid-pack tomatoes
2 cans (6 ounces each) tomato sauce
2 whole bay leaves
½ teaspoon dried oregano
¼ teaspoon dried basil
  Salt and coarsely ground black pepper, to taste
2 cups dry white wine
1 pound prawns, cooked, shelled, deveined
2 pounds uncooked sea trout, bass, rock cod or other firm fish, skinned and boned, cut in bite-size pieces
3 or 4 cooked Dungeness crabs

Heat oil slowly in a large, deep, heavy kettle. Chop onion, parsley and garlic together until fine. Sauté in oil until lightly browned. Add tomatoes, tomato sauce, bay leaves, oregano and basil; add salt and pepper to taste. Simmer gently, covered, for 1 hour. Add wine, prawns and fish. Cook 20 minutes, stirring occasionally. Crack crab claws, leaving meat in shells; remove remaining meat from crabs. Put crab meat and cracked claws in kettle; correct seasoning and cook another 10 minutes to heat through. Serve in soup plates.

Ann McDuffie

The Tampa Tribune / Tampa, Florida

Potaje de Garbanzos, or Spanish Bean Soup, is very popular here in Spanish restaurants. The soup is served on the streets of Ybor City, Tampa's Latin Quarter, during the Gasparilla Festival Week in February. Tourists love it. It's also tinted green for St. Patrick's Day! And even though I hate tinted foods, I get a kick out of green garbanzo soup.

This recipe is from Clara Garcia, wife of the second-generation owner of Las Novedades Restaurant, which no longer exists in Ybor City. She also authored the cookbook, Clarita's Cocina *(Clara's Kitchen). This is her personal recipe, one her restaurateur husband liked.*

POTAJE DE GARBANZOS

6 generous servings

1 pound dried garbanzos (chick peas)
  Water
  Salt
½ pound smoked bacon
1 ham bone (½ pound)
½ pound lean beef (flank)
2 chorizos (Spanish sausages), or 4 to 5 inches kielbasa
1 small whole onion
½ green pepper
1 whole ripe tomato
1 bay leaf
  Pinch saffron
3 medium potatoes, peeled and cubed

Wash beans in cold water. Discard imperfect ones. Cover with salted water at least 3 inches above beans. Soak overnight. The next morning, drain and rinse beans thoroughly. Set beans aside.

Place bacon, ham bone, beef, chorizos, onion, green pepper, tomato and bay leaf in a 3- to 4-quart saucepan or soup pot. Cover with water 2 inches above ingredients. Bring to a rapid boil; skim several times. Lower heat to moderate, cover, and place saffron on the cover to toast. Cook about 30 minutes

Add beans and bring to a boil again. Cover and reduce heat to moderate; cook another 30 minutes. Crumble toasted saffron and add. Stir gently once. Cover and cook another 30 minutes, or until beans are tender and not overcooked.

By this time, meats should be tender. Remove meats to heated platter and reserve. Discard ham bone and remainder of onion, green pepper, tomato and bay leaf.

Add potatoes to beans and correct salt seasoning. Cover and cook over moderate heat until potatoes are done, about 30 minutes.

Cut beef into small portions. Slice chorizos into thin rings. Cube the cooked bacon. Return meats to soup kettle. Heat thoroughly and serve hot.

Note: Tampans make a full lunch on this soup with salad and hot Cuban bread with butter. Others could substitute crusty Italian or French bread for the Cuban bread. I have served it as a main dish at night with a "galumptuous" flan (custard with burnt sugar topping) for dessert, a meal my husband loved.

One of my fond memories of growing up in Green Bay, Wisconsin, and spending summers at a cottage along the Bay shore of Lake Michigan is the special weekends when the men in the family decided to cook a huge kettle of booyah. It would bubble all day long over an open fire, sending a tantalizing aroma over the area and bringing the children in the family to the kettle often, anxious for the men to begin serving it in huge white bowls.

On summer Sundays in later years, we frequented Belgian taverns, where the thick soup was cooked in outdoor summer kitchens. Ladled into the familiar pristine bowls, the soup was enjoyed around picnic tables and eaten with crackers and mugs of cool beer.

The recipe came from a friend of my mother; she has brewed many a pot to feed an army of friends, who seem to be always present at the cottage in northern Wisconsin.

CHICKEN BOOYAH
4 gallons

5 pounds stewing chicken, cut up
1½ pounds beef stew meat
¼ pound lean pork, cubed
½ pound dried navy beans, soaked overnight
½ pound split green peas
2 cups canned whole tomatoes
4 cups diced carrots
2½ cups diced onions
3 cups diced celery
½ lemon, peeled and cut into pieces
8 cups diced potatoes
4 cups shredded cabbage
4 tablespoons butter
Salt and pepper, to taste

Place cut-up chicken, beef stew meat and pork in a large soup kettle. Cover with cold water. Slowly bring to a boil. Skim. Simmer 1 hour.

Add drained navy beans, green peas, tomatoes, carrots, onions, celery and lemon. Cook about 3 hours, or until chicken is very tender.

Add potatoes, cabbage, butter, salt and pepper. Simmer 30 minutes.

Note: During cooking, it will be necessary to add cold water to keep meats and vegetables covered and to ensure a soup that is not too thick.

Evelyn Wavpotich

The Island Packet / Hilton Head Island, South Carolina

Peanut soup is a Southern specialty. This version is from Dotty Cason, who studied at the Cordon Bleu in Paris but likes cooking the Southern way, too.

CREAMY PEANUT SOUP

10 to 12 servings

¼ cup butter or margarine
1 medium onion, chopped
2 ribs celery, chopped into
    small pieces
3 tablespoons all-purpose
    flour
8 cups canned or homemade
    chicken broth

2 cups creamy peanut butter
1¾ to 2 cups light cream or
    half-and-half
⅓ cup chopped peanuts
    (unsalted), for garnish
    Paprika, for garnish

Melt butter in a large pan. When butter is bubbly, stir in onion and celery; cook until clear but not browned. Add flour and stir until well mixed. Pour in chicken broth; blend well, stirring constantly, and bring to a boil. Turn down heat and add peanut butter, stirring until blended.

Put soup through a sieve. Add cream slowly to the strained soup and stir for a few minutes to blend.

Pour soup into small bowls (it's very rich); garnish with chopped peanuts and dash of paprika for color.

The Cobb Salad has been a Los Angeles tradition ever since it was created by the Original Hollywood Brown Derby restaurant. With the advent of the food processor, it's easier to prepare at home. This main-course salad is marvelous for luncheon parties. The unassembled salad is usually presented at the table and then tossed, because it is most attractive before tossing.

THE ORIGINAL HOLLYWOOD BROWN DERBY COBB SALAD

6 servings

½ head iceberg lettuce
½ bunch watercress
1 small bunch curly endive
½ head romaine lettuce
2 tablespoons minced chives
2 medium tomatoes, peeled, seeded and diced
1 whole chicken breast, cooked, boned, skinned and diced

6 slices bacon, cooked and diced
1 avocado, peeled and diced
3 hard-cooked eggs, peeled and diced
⅓ cup Roquefort cheese, crumbled
French Dressing (recipe follows)

Chop lettuce, watercress, endive and romaine in very fine pieces using a knife or a food processor. Mix chopped ingredients together in one large wide bowl, or in individual wide shallow bowls. Add chives. Arrange tomatoes, chicken, bacon, avocado and eggs in narrow strips or wedges across top of greens. Sprinkle with cheese. Chill.

At serving time, toss with ½ cup French Dressing. Pass remaining dressing.

FRENCH DRESSING

1½ cups

¼ cup water
¼ cup red wine vinegar
¼ teaspoon granulated sugar
1½ teaspoons lemon juice
½ teaspoon salt
½ teaspoon black pepper

½ teaspoon Worcestershire sauce
¾ teaspoon dry mustard
½ clove garlic, minced
¼ cup olive oil
¾ cup vegetable oil

Combine water, vinegar, sugar, lemon juice, salt, pepper, Worcestershire sauce, mustard, garlic and oils in a container with lid. Shake well before using.

Jann Malone

Richmond Times-Dispatch / Richmond, Virginia

If ever a dish were misnamed, this is it, because the eggs are just a garnish for a glorious crab and shrimp salad with a spicy vinaigrette dressing. The Pontchartrain part of the name is right—the dish comes from New Orleans, which is next to Lake Pontchartrain.

Kolb's, a German restaurant in New Orleans, serves this salad to customers who are savvy enough to know what they're ordering. I devised this recipe from my recollections of how the salad tasted.

EGGS PONTCHARTRAIN

2 servings

Lettuce
1 pound crab meat
½ pound shrimp, cooked and
    peeled
2 hard-cooked eggs, peeled
2 tomatoes

Dressing:
1 clove garlic
½ teaspoon salt
½ teaspoon pepper
½ teaspoon granulated sugar
1 tablespoon Creole mustard
    (see note)
3 tablespoons red wine
    vinegar
½ cup vegetable oil

Line two plates with lettuce. Put half of crab meat in the center of each plate. Arrange shrimp around crab meat. Slice eggs into thin circles and place egg slices on top of crab meat. Slice tomatoes and arrange tomato slices around the outside of the plates.

Prepare dressing by crushing garlic in a small bowl. Add salt, pepper, sugar and mustard; stir to make a paste. Blend in vinegar. Slowly whisk in oil. Pour dressing over the salad. Serve immediately.

Note: Creole mustard is a brown, spicy mustard available in the specialty food section of most supermarkets. Dijon mustard is a fine substitute.

Jane Baker

The Phoenix Gazette / Phoenix, Arizona

Jicama is a not-so-pretty root vegetable whose popularity has spread from Mexico to the Southwest. It is available in Phoenix supermarkets from November to July. Despite its outward appearance, jicama is quite tasty—something of a cross between a potato, an apple and a water chestnut. It's low in calories (only forty-five calories per medium jicama) and low in sodium. Sticks of jicama rolled in chili powder often are sold by street vendors in Mexico. I like to use jicama in this salad.

JICAMA SALAD
6 servings

1 medium jicama, peeled and
    cut into strips
1 small red onion, cut into
    rings
1 cucumber, sliced
3 large seedless oranges,
    peeled and cut into
    sections

⅓ cup lime juice
¼ cup vegetable oil
½ to 1 teaspoon chili powder
1 clove garlic, chopped

Prepare jicama strips, onion rings, cucumber slices and orange sections; arrange on individual plates, or toss together in a salad bowl.

Combine lime juice, oil, chili powder and garlic in a small container; mix well. The amount of chili powder varies according to how spicy you like your food. Drizzle dressing over salad.

Karen K. Marshall

St. Louis Globe-Democrat / St. Louis, Missouri

This Italian salad was originally served at Rich and Charlie's Pasta House, a local restaurant. It is now served at all the Pasta House Company restaurants and has become more or less classic fare for St. Louisans, whether dining out or at home.

ITALIAN SALAD
6 servings

1 head iceberg lettuce,
    shredded
⅓ head romaine lettuce,
    shredded
1 pimiento, chopped
1 jar (6 ounces) artichoke
    hearts, drained

¾ cup olive oil
¼ cup vinegar
¼ cup grated Parmesan cheese
Salt and pepper, to taste
Additional grated Parmesan
    cheese, for garnish

Combine iceberg and romaine lettuces in a salad bowl. Add pimiento and artichoke hearts. Toss well.

Combine oil, vinegar and ¼ cup Parmesan cheese in a shaker; mix well. Coat salad greens generously with the dressing. Add salt and pepper to taste.

Serve generous portions on individual plates; garnish with additional Parmesan cheese.

Peggy Daum
The Milwaukee Journal / Milwaukee, Wisconsin

In many restaurants in the Milwaukee area, spinach salad with hot bacon dressing is a specialty. The idea originated with the city's German population, but the recipe has spread far beyond German homes and restaurants.

Sometimes the dressing is used with a mixture of spinach and lettuce. And in summertime, when home cooks pour the dressing over tender leaf lettuce from the garden, the combination is known as wilted lettuce.

Proportions for the dressing vary with the chef or cook. At some restaurants, the dressing is thickened. This version comes from Jim Hahm, who grows lots of lettuce in his side-yard garden.

SPINACH SALAD WITH HOT BACON DRESSING

4 to 6 servings

2 bunches (about 1 pound) untrimmed fresh spinach
6 slices bacon, diced

¼ cup white vinegar
¼ cup granulated sugar

Wash spinach and remove stems. Drain and spin or wrap in toweling to dry.

Fry diced bacon in a skillet over medium-high heat until crisp. Remove from heat and pour off half the grease (or more if desired), leaving ¼ cup or less in pan. Stir in vinegar and sugar.

Tear spinach into bite-size pieces and place in a heat-proof salad bowl.

Bring dressing mixture to a boil over high heat. Pour over salad and toss. Serve immediately. (It is important to serve and eat this salad quickly because the bacon fat congeals as it cools.)

Peggy Daum

The Milwaukee Journal / Milwaukee, Wisconsin

This warm salad is so much a part of Milwaukee that it seems to be on the table at every family gathering, church supper, club potluck, company picnic—you name it. It's also found at deli counters and on restaurant salad bars.

I was eleven or so before I knew that any other kind of potato salad existed. That's when I saw an egg-and-mayonnaise version at a Girl Scout potluck supper and said, "What funny potato salad!"

Unfortunately, I was speaking to the Scout whose mother had prepared it.

I've learned to like a number of potato salads since, but German Potato Salad is still my favorite.

GERMAN POTATO SALAD

8 to 10 servings

3 pounds small red potatoes
1 bunch green onions, chopped (tops included)
6 slices bacon, diced
3 tablespoons all-purpose flour
½ cup granulated sugar
1½ teaspoons salt, or to taste
¼ teaspoon pepper
1 cup cider vinegar
1 cup water
1 tablespoon chopped fresh parsley (optional)

Wash potatoes but do not peel. Place in a kettle with water to cover. Cover and boil over medium heat just until tender, about 20 minutes. Do not overcook; potatoes should not be mushy. Drain and cool slightly for easier handling. Peel potatoes and cut in thin slices. Place in a large bowl. Add onions to potatoes. Cover and set aside.

Fry diced bacon in a skillet over medium heat until crisp. Remove from heat. Remove bacon with a slotted spoon and drain on paper towels, reserving drippings in skillet. Add bacon to potatoes.

Combine flour, sugar, salt and pepper in a small bowl. Add to bacon drippings in skillet and stir over medium heat to form a smooth paste. Stir in vinegar and water. Bring to a boil and boil 2 to 3 minutes, stirring constantly.

Pour hot sauce over potatoes, onions and bacon. Mix gently. If desired, sprinkle with parsley before serving.

Main Dishes

Jann Malone

Richmond Times-Dispatch / Richmond, Virginia

This recipe is a favorite with Virginia cooks. The seasonings are subdued, so the subtle crab flavor will still come through.

CRAB IMPERIAL
4 servings

3 tablespoons butter
3 tablespoons all-purpose flour
1 cup milk
1 teaspoon dry mustard
1 teaspoon Worcestershire sauce
2 tablespoons mayonnaise
1 pound crab meat

Make a white sauce by slowly melting butter over low heat in a medium saucepan. Add flour and stir with a whisk for 3 to 4 minutes (this eliminates the taste of raw flour). Slowly add milk; simmer and stir with a wire whisk until sauce has thickened and is smooth.

Combine dry mustard, Worcestershire sauce and mayonnaise in a small bowl; mix well. Add mayonnaise mixture to white sauce.

Gently mix crab meat with white sauce mixture, taking care not to break up crab meat. Spoon mixture into individual crab shells or ramekins or a 1-quart casserole dish. Bake in a preheated 350°F oven 20 minutes, or until bubbly.

Jann Malone

Richmond Times-Dispatch / Richmond, Virginia

When she heard me complaining about too much breading in crab cakes, Ruth Ramsay gave me her recipe. As you can see, it has very little bread in it. She uses claw crab meat.

CRAB CAKES
2 to 4 servings

1 pound crab meat
1 tablespoon mayonnaise
1 egg, beaten
Salt and pepper, to taste
Worcestershire sauce, to taste
Fresh bread crumbs
4 to 6 tablespoons butter

Mix crab meat, mayonnaise, egg, salt, pepper and Worcestershire sauce; form into cakes. (The smaller you make the cakes, the better they hold together.) Dip both sides of each cake in bread crumbs.

Melt butter in a skillet. Cook crab cakes in butter over moderate heat until heated through and lightly browned.

Jane Benet

San Francisco Chronicle / San Francisco, California

Hangtown Fry comes from the Gold Country in California's Sierra foothills, but it is served in old San Francisco restaurants still.

There are several stories about the origin of the dish, and this one seems most plausible:

A gold miner, a Forty-Niner, came to town (town being today's Placerville, which was then, for fairly obvious reasons, called Hangtown) with a sack of gold nuggets. He walked into the first restaurant he saw and demanded that the cook prepare the most expensive thing he had in the house, spilling the nuggets onto the counter to prove he could pay.

Since oysters had to travel all the way from the East Coast in barrels in those days, and since eggs were scarcer than hens' teeth in the Sierra foothill town, those two items were the most expensive ones on hand, so the cook dished them up in the original Hangtown Fry.

HANGTOWN FRY
4 servings

9 eggs, divided
Salt and pepper, to taste
8 medium-size oysters
Bread crumbs
Butter

4 link sausages
4 lamb kidneys
4 slices bacon
Parsley

Beat 1 egg in a shallow bowl with a little salt and pepper. Dip oysters in beaten egg, then in bread crumbs; sauté in butter until plump and golden. Remove and drain on paper towels.

Put link sausages in a small heavy pan and add a few drops of water. Cover and cook slowly until browned. Set aside.

Split lamb kidneys in half, remove membranes, then place on a rack with the bacon and broil, turning once, until bacon is crisp and kidneys are done to your liking. Set aside.

Beat remaining 8 eggs with salt and pepper to taste. Melt some butter in a medium pan and pour one-fourth of egg mixture into it when it is hot. Arrange 2 oysters, 1 sausage, 2 kidney halves and 1 slice of bacon in the egg in pan. Cook as you would any omelet, but don't roll it; then finish the last-minute cooking under the broiler. Serve immediately, garnished with fresh parsley, or keep warm in a low oven while you cook the other three omelets.

Fran H. Zupan

The Columbia Record / Columbia, South Carolina

According to Eva Anderson, a staff writer, this is an old Charleston recipe that has been handed down through the generations.

SCALLOPED OYSTERS

4 to 6 servings

½ cup butter or margarine, melted
1 cup crushed salted soda crackers
½ cup dry bread crumbs
1 pint fresh shucked oysters (reserve liquid)

Salt
Paprika
6 tablespoons light or heavy cream, or more, as needed
2 tablespoons butter or margarine

Combine melted butter, crushed crackers and bread crumbs. Place half of crumb mixture in a greased 8-inch square pan. Cover with oysters, being careful to remove any shells. Sprinkle lightly with salt and paprika. Top with remaining crumb mixture.

Combine oyster liquid with cream to make ½ cup. Pour over crumbs. Dot with butter. Bake in a preheated 400°F oven 25 to 30 minutes, or until top is nicely browned.

Jane Benet

San Francisco Chronicle / San Francisco, California

Oyster loaf is an old, old San Francisco favorite. The dish used to be served in restaurants all over the city but is much harder to come by now, so we most often make our own. It may be made with a standard long loaf of bread, but traditionally it is prepared using a round loaf.

OYSTER LOAF

6 to 8 servings

1 fresh round loaf sourdough
    French bread
½ cup butter, or more
24 medium-size oysters

Fine dry bread crumbs
Salt and pepper
Fresh lemon juice
Chopped fresh parsley

Cut off top of loaf of bread about two-thirds of the way up. Scoop out center of loaf and top, leaving a 1-inch crust all around. (Either dry the scooped-out bread in the oven and make it into fine crumbs, or reserve it for another use.) Melt butter in a skillet and use to paint inside of loaf (and top) generously. Toast loaf lightly in a 400°F oven 5 to 10 minutes.

Add more butter to that you've melted, if necessary, for frying oysters. Drain oysters, then coat lightly with fine dry bread crumbs, adding salt and pepper to taste. Cook oysters in butter in a skillet just until golden and plump.

Now, layer fried oysters into buttered loaf, sprinkling lightly with fresh lemon juice and chopped fresh parsley as you go. Place top back on loaf, paint outside with butter, place on a baking sheet and pop into a 400°F oven 8 to 10 minutes.

Serve with thin slices of dill pickle (or French cornichons) and any favorite dunking sauce for oysters—or plain.

Note: To serve and eat Oyster Loaf, it really is best to break the loaf into chunks, being sure each diner gets his or her share of the plump oysters. Then eat it out of hand—or use forks, if you're fussy.

Editor's note: Oyster Loaf is also a New Orleans favorite. You'll find it in many bars and small restaurants there.

Evelyn Wavpotich

The Island Packet / Hilton Head Island, South Carolina

South Carolina Governor Dick Riley's wife, Ann, enjoys cooking, but, understandably, doesn't have much time to spend in the kitchen. And, of course, she doesn't have to when they're at the Governor's Mansion. She created this tasty regional dish.

COLONIAL OYSTER AND HAM PIE   *4 generous servings*

1 pint fresh oysters
½ cup butter
½ cup all-purpose flour
½ cup white wine
½ cup milk

1 medium onion, chopped
2 teaspoons butter
1½ cups diced, cooked ham
2 cups canned or frozen
   green peas

Drain fresh oysters and reserve ½ cup oyster liquor. Melt the ½ cup butter in a saucepan; stir in flour. Add reserved oyster liquor, white wine and milk. Cook until thick. Remove from heat. Cook onion until soft in 2 teaspoons butter; add to liquid mixture along with drained oysters, ham and peas. Turn mixture into a 2-quart casserole dish. Bake in a preheated 400°F oven 15 minutes.

Helen Wilber Richardson

The Providence Journal-Bulletin / Providence, Rhode Island

These are an extremely popular item at shore restaurants in Rhode Island.

RHODE ISLAND CLAM CAKES
6 *servings*

¼ cup liquid from clams
1 egg, well beaten
1 cup all-purpose flour
1 teaspoon baking powder
½ teaspoon salt

1 cup chopped quahogs (large, hard-shelled clams; see note)
Vegetable oil for frying

Combine clam liquid, beaten egg, flour, baking powder and salt in a medium mixing bowl. Mix well, then stir in chopped clams and mix well again.

Heat 3 or 4 inches of oil in heavy pan. Drop batter by teaspoonful into oil. Fry until golden brown, 4 to 6 minutes.

Note: For those without access to quahogs, substitute two cans (7 ounces each) minced clams. Drain very well, reserving ¼ cup liquid, as called for in ingredients.

Barbara Durbin

The Oregonian / Portland, Oregon

When you say "fish" in the Northwest, the first one to come to mind is salmon. It should be cooked only until flaky but still moist, not until it's dry.

The West Coast Fisheries Development Foundation sponsored a grilled seafood contest in Portland in 1983. This stuffed salmon recipe, entered by Deborah McGuire of Lake Oswego, placed third.

GRILLED RICE-STUFFED SALMON

6 servings

½ cup diced onion
½ cup diced celery
½ cup diced green pepper
4 cloves garlic, or garlic powder, to taste
3 tablespoons butter
1 cup sliced fresh mushrooms
2 cups cooked rice

½ cup sliced olives
½ cup chopped fresh parsley
3 tablespoons fresh basil, or dried basil, to taste
1 salmon (6 to 8 pounds), head removed
1 lemon, thinly sliced

Sauté onion, celery, green pepper and garlic in butter in a skillet for 3 minutes. Add mushrooms. Add sautéed vegetables to rice; add olives, parsley and basil.

Place salmon on heavy-duty aluminum foil. Stuff salmon with lemon slices and rice mixture. (Any remaining rice may also be wrapped in foil and grilled.) Wrap securely. Grill over medium coals 30 minutes to 1 hour.

Charlotte Hansen

The Jamestown Sun / Jamestown, North Dakota

This Norwegian favorite is popular among ethnic groups in North Dakota.

LUTEFISK

Lutefisk
Salted water

Salt, to taste
Butter

Remove any bones or skin on lutefisk. Cut fish into serving pieces. Soak overnight in salted water. Take directly out of water (do not rinse) and place on aluminum foil. Season with salt and butter, then wrap in foil. Bake in a 350°F oven 30 minutes.

Serve lutefisk with melted butter and boiled potatoes, if desired.

Note: Lutefisk is codfish that has been dried, then soaked first in water, then in lye or chemicals, then again in water. After this, it is cooked.

Carol Haddix

Chicago Tribune / Chicago, Illinois

The following dish was said to have originated in De Jonghe's, a traditional Chicago restaurant at the turn of the century which is now defunct. The dish, however, lives on in many other Chicago restaurants and across the country.

SHRIMP DE JONGHE

8 to 10 servings

1 small onion, sliced
2 celery tops
6 peppercorns
1 bay leaf
1¾ teaspoons salt, divided
4 pounds medium shrimp in the shell
1 cup butter, melted, divided

¼ cup dry sherry
3 cups fine fresh bread crumbs
¼ cup minced parsley
1 clove garlic, crushed
½ teaspoon paprika
Dash cayenne

Heat 3 quarts water, onion, celery, peppercorns, bay leaf and 1 teaspoon salt to boiling in a large saucepot. Add shrimp; cover and return to a boil. Drain shrimp and peel. Toss shrimp in a large bowl with ½ cup melted butter and sherry; set aside.

Combine bread crumbs and remaining ½ cup melted butter. Stir in parsley, remaining ¾ teaspoon salt, garlic, paprika and cayenne.

Spoon half of shrimp mixture into a 2-quart casserole. Sprinkle with half of bread crumb mixture. Top with remaining shrimp mixture and remaining bread crumb mixture. Bake in a 350°F oven 45 to 55 minutes, until crumbs are lightly browned and shrimp is tender.

Morning Advocate and State-Times / Baton Rouge, Louisiana

Etouffée means smothered. Shrimp or Crawfish Etouffée is not only a South Louisiana favorite, but it also is a quick dish, made from scratch in just a few minutes.

SHRIMP OR CRAWFISH ETOUFFEE

4 to 6 servings

½ cup butter or margarine
1½ tablespoons all-purpose flour
¾ cup chopped celery
¾ cup chopped green pepper
¾ cup chopped onion
1 pound peeled, uncooked shrimp, or 1 pound uncooked crawfish tails
Salt, black pepper and cayenne, to taste
¼ cup chopped green onion tops
¼ cup chopped fresh parsley
Hot cooked rice

Melt butter in a large skillet. Add flour and lightly brown it. Add celery, green pepper and onion; cook until tender, stirring occasionally. Add shrimp or crawfish tails. Cover and cook 15 minutes on low heat, stirring occasionally. Add salt, pepper and cayenne to taste. Add onion tops and parsley. Simmer a few minutes, covered, to blend seasonings. Serve over rice.

Note: For extra gravy, add ¼ cup vermouth, white wine or chicken broth with onion tops and parsley. Stir well.

Louise Dodd

The Courier Herald / Dublin, Georgia

We were served this recipe at an old inn on Cumberland Island, off the coast of Georgia. The inn was formerly the home of Andrew Carnegie and was run by his grandchildren. The hostess willingly shared it, and I have enjoyed serving this dish many times at parties. It's very simple, but oh, such a delicious main course on a hot Georgia night.

CUMBERLAND ISLAND SHRIMP

8 to 10 servings

5 pounds shrimp
½ teaspoon garlic powder
5 to 10 whole cloves
3 cups cooked rice
2 ribs celery, cut into small pieces
1 onion, grated (save juices from grating)
1 green pepper, finely chopped
1 cup mayonnaise
  Curry powder, to taste
  Lettuce, tomatoes, sliced cucumbers, for garnish (optional)

Cook shrimp very quickly (for only a few minutes) in water to cover, in a large kettle, with garlic powder and cloves. Drain, peel and chop or break into pieces. Reserve a few whole shrimp to use for garnish, if desired.

Combine chopped shrimp, rice, celery, onion and onion juices, green pepper, mayonnaise and curry powder in a bowl. Toss lightly. This may be served as is, or may be placed in a lightly oiled fish mold and then turned out on a platter.

This is attractive when garnished simply with lettuce, tomatoes, sliced cucumbers and a few reserved whole shrimp.

Evelyn Wavpotich

The Island Packet / Hilton Head Island, South Carolina

This is a recipe that is so simple and quick, so flexible for stretching, and so ideal for any occasion that it belongs in everyone's file.

At our last family reunion, my husband took down our largest pot from a high shelf, filled it with water, and within half an hour we feasted on the three main ingredients. As former Northerners, we latched on to this Carolina recipe really fast.

LOW-COUNTRY BOIL

2 tablespoons **crab and shrimp boil** (seasoning mixture available in most supermarkets)
   Hot (or mild) **Polish-type sausage**, cut into 1-inch pieces
   Corn on the cob, broken in half (allow one ear per person)
   Raw, unpeeled **shrimp** (allow ½ pound per person)

Fill a large pot with enough water to cover ingredients. Add crab and shrimp boil. When water comes to a boil, add sausage and corn. Boil 10 minutes. Add shrimp. Boil 2 to 3 minutes, until shrimp turns pink. (Long cooking toughens shrimp.) Remove and drain sausage, corn and shrimp.

Note: Shrimp is served unpeeled, and everyone peels his own. This adds to the fun. Of course, the host or hostess can attend to this chore, if preferred, for a neater party. Be sure to have melted butter available for the corn and a sauce (usually a mixture of ketchup and horseradish) for dipping the shrimp. Cole slaw and beer complete the menu.

The Scandinavian fishermen who came to Door County—the "thumb" of Wisconsin that juts into Lake Michigan—are credited with starting the custom of the fish boil. For them, the fish boil was a necessity, a way to cook part of the day's catch for supper.

Today, for the tourists who flock to Door County in the summertime, the fish boil is a popular attraction, a spectacular show—and a tasty supper. It's staged by many of the restaurants and hotels that dot the vacationland.

Fish, potatoes and, usually, onions are boiled in a large kettle of salted water over a wood fire. When they're ready for eating, the boilmaster adds kerosene to the fire. The flames shoot up, the show is dramatic and the pot boils over, carrying off the fish fat that has accumulated on the water.

The boiled dinner is completed, traditionally, with cole slaw, rye bread and cherry pie—made from Door County's tart cherry crop, of course.

A home-size version of a fish boil can be done in any very large kettle, but one with a removable basket is helpful.

The following recipe is adapted from one worked out for home cooks by Phillip and Rosemary Voight, owners of the Viking Restaurant in Ellison Bay, which claims to have Door County's oldest and largest fish boil.

DOOR COUNTY FISH BOIL

8 servings

16 small onions
16 small red potatoes
½ pound non-iodized salt, divided

16 chunks whitefish (7 to 8 pounds)
8 lemon wedges, for garnish
¾ cup melted butter

Peel onions. Wash potatoes and slice a small piece off ends, but do not peel.

Bring 2 gallons water to a boil in a large kettle. Add ¼ pound of the salt and bring to a boil again. Add potatoes and boil, uncovered, 16 minutes. Add onions and boil, uncovered, 4 minutes longer.

If insert basket is available, place fish in basket. Add fish and remaining ¼ pound salt. Boil, uncovered, 10 minutes longer.

Remove from heat. Skim off any fish oil that accumulated during cooking. Drain into a colander. Place fish and vegetables on a serving platter or individual plates; garnish with lemon wedges. Serve with melted butter.

Note: A large quantity of salt is traditional in this recipe. The amount may be reduced, if desired.

Diane Wiggins
St. Louis Globe-Democrat / St. Louis, Missouri

Although I work in St. Louis, I live in a rural area near Belleville, Illinois, across the Mississippi River. Belleville and the smaller surrounding towns have a tradition of Friday fish fries that I have not found in other areas, even as near as St. Louis. The tradition probably stems from the Catholic practice of abstaining from meat during the Fridays of Lent. Gradually, the serving of fish as an alternative entrée became extended to every Friday.

On Friday nights, many taverns, schools, churches and community groups, such as VFWs, sponsor fish fries that are open to the public. A few private entrepreneurs operate small family-run weekend fish stands that do a landslide business, especially during warm weather, when you can eat on picnic tables in outdoor beer gardens attached to the stands. Carryouts are popular.

The food is generally good, reasonable in price and served on heavy paper plates. A cold beer is the standard accompaniment, with sodas for the kids. The menu is limited, generally, to deep-fried squares of cod served on white or rye bread, with tartar sauce, cole slaw and French fries. A few places also offer catfish, jack salmon and, if you want to get fancy, shrimp. Cut-ups, chunks of fish deep-fried and accompanied by bread, are available by the plate or the pound. Non-fish lovers can get a hamburger or, sometimes, pizza.

Here is a recipe for fried fish the way my mother, Dorothy Raab, makes it. She uses the bluegill or bass she and my father catch in local lakes. The fish are filleted into boneless pieces that are dipped in batter and deep-fried.

BEER-BATTERED FISH   *4 servings*

1 **cup buttermilk baking mix**
1 **cup beer** (your favorite brand)
   Garlic salt, salt and pepper, to taste
2 **to 3 pounds of fillets** (the catch of the day, cleaned and filleted)
   Vegetable oil for frying

Combine baking mix, beer, garlic salt, salt and pepper in a bowl. Dip cleaned fish fillets in batter. Fry in hot oil in a deep-fryer or skillet until golden brown. Drain on absorbent towels. Serve hot.

Marian Burros

The New York Times / New York, New York

This recipe for Maryland stuffed ham is from a story I did in a magazine. A woman named Alice Shorter, who lives in southern Maryland, showed me how to do it.

Traditionally, a country ham is used in this recipe, but we found that regular ham works very well. Because this ham should be cooled in the broth in which it has been cooked, you may wish to prepare the ham the day before it is to be served.

SOUTHERN MARYLAND STUFFED HAM   *15 servings*

   2 large, green cabbages (about 3 pounds each), cored and finely
      chopped
1½ pounds kale, finely chopped
   3 medium onions, finely chopped
   4 ribs celery, finely chopped
 ½ teaspoon cayenne
 ½ teaspoon pepper
   1 teaspoon dry mustard
   1 precooked bone-in ham (about 10 pounds)

For stuffing: Place cabbage, kale, onions, celery, cayenne, pepper and mustard in a large stockpot; add water to within 1 inch of the top of vegetables and, stirring occasionally, bring to a boil over moderate heat. Turn off heat, cover the pot and let vegetables rest for 10 minutes in the hot water. Pour vegetables into a colander set over a bowl to catch the broth. Reserve broth; cool vegetables to room temperature.

To stuff ham: Cut an "X" measuring 1 inch square and 2 inches deep on underside of ham. Fill "X" with vegetable stuffing until no more will fit. Continue cutting "X's" about ½- to 1-inch apart all over ham, stuffing them as they are cut. Center ham on a 4-foot-long piece of double-thickness cheesecloth and place any remaining stuffing on top of ham. Wrap cheesecloth around ham and tie ends together to hold stuffing in place.

To cook ham: Return ham to the stockpot along with reserved broth; add enough water to cover ham. Place lid on pot and bring liquid to a boil over high heat. Reduce heat to low and continue to cook ham for 2 hours, adding water as needed to keep ham covered. Remove pot from heat and allow ham to cool for an hour in the cooking broth. Then transfer ham to a large colander or a rack to drain for about 1 hour. Remove and discard cheesecloth and place any extra vegetable stuffing on top of ham in a serving dish. To serve, slice ham and accompany with vegetable stuffing.

Bernie Arnold
Nashville Banner / Nashville, Tennessee

We're sure this recipe would work just as well with country hams from other parts of the United States. It's just that we've never cooked hams from West Virginia, North Dakota, Georgia, etc., etc.

HOW TO COOK A TENNESSEE COUNTRY HAM

In the morning, scrub **ham** with a stiff brush; soak all day in cold water. In the evening, lift out and put on stove in a large container with a good top. Pour hot water in container until ham is covered. Add to water:

1 cup pickle juice, or ½ cup
  cider vinegar
1 red (hot) pepper, seeds
  removed

1 lemon, quartered
1 onion, cut in half
2 bay leaves

Put top on tight and turn stove on high. When a rolling boil is reached, cook for 1 hour. Cut off stove and cover lid with thick newspapers (preferably the *Nashville Banner*).

Cover all with a woolen blanket and tie around sides to keep heat in. Let stay on the "cut off" stove until morning.

When ham is cool enough to handle, lift out bone, skin the rind and lightly pierce the fat side. Rub in **2 teaspoons prepared mustard.** Pat on **brown sugar** and **bread crumbs.** Pour **½ cup sherry** over top of ham. Stick with **whole cloves.**

Brown in oven. Watch carefully so as not to burn. Let cool *overnight* before slicing thin. (The last step is very important.)

Elaine Corn

The Courier-Journal / Louisville, Kentucky

Country Ham is a classic in Kentucky. The term "red-eye" supposedly comes from the little red circles or "eyes" of grease that form in the gravy on the plate.

COUNTRY HAM AND RED-EYE GRAVY
8 to 10 servings

Vegetable oil
8 slices (¼-inch thickness) raw
   country ham

¾ cup black coffee
1 teaspoon granulated sugar

Heat a few drops of oil in a large skillet until skillet is medium hot. Lay ham slices in skillet. Cook on one side for 8 minutes over medium-high heat. Turn slices and fry 8 minutes more. Pour coffee into skillet with ham slices. Sprinkle with sugar and stir. Cover and let simmer over very low heat for 5 to 10 minutes. Serve ham and red-eye gravy together.

Sandra Day

The Times-Picayune/States-Item / New Orleans, Louisiana

This is a traditional Monday dish in New Orleans. It started out as a way to use the ham bone left over after Sunday dinner. The beans could be put on the back of the stove to cook all day, since Monday was wash day. All of the cafeterias still have this for luncheon plates on Monday.

RED BEANS AND RICE
4 to 6 servings

1 pound dried red beans or
   kidney beans
1 quart hot water
1 large ham bone with meat
1 large onion, chopped
½ cup chopped green onion
2 cloves garlic, pressed

1 bay leaf
½ teaspoon cayenne
1½ teaspoons salt
1 pound smoked sausage, cut
   into 1-inch pieces
Hot cooked rice

Sort beans and rinse well; cover with tap water and soak overnight. Drain beans and place in a large heavy pot; add hot water, ham bone, onion, green onion, garlic, bay leaf, cayenne and salt. Bring mixture to a boil; cover and reduce heat. Simmer beans 2 hours, or until tender, adding more water if necessary to keep from sticking; stir often.

Add sausage to beans and simmer, uncovered, about 15 minutes longer, or until a thick gravy forms; stir occasionally. Serve over rice.

Scrapple (a Pennsylvania Dutch specialty) and its next of kin, Goetta, are exactly the same thing, except that while Scrapple is thickened with cornmeal, Goetta is thickened with pin (also called cross-cut) oats. Goetta, fried like cornmeal mush, is found on Cincinnati restaurant breakfast menus.

These dishes have a long history that goes back to midwinter butchering time on farms. Scrappy bits of fresh pork were simmered in water with seasonings until the meat would easily come off the bones. After the meat was removed from the bones, it was finely chopped or put through a food grinder. Then the mixture of meat and broth was brought to boiling and thickened with cornmeal or pin oats and poured into pans to chill.

It was kept in a cold place for a couple of weeks or longer before it was sliced and cooked on a griddle or skillet until golden brown and crusty. Drenched with maple syrup, it made (and still does) a dish fit for the gods. Don't forget—Scrapple and Goetta are as good at lunch or supper as for breakfast.

Goetta is similar to chili in that everyone has his or her own version. This version comes from Fern Storer, former food editor.

GOETTA   *5 to 6 servings (18 slices)*

1 pound high-grade pork sausage
1 quart water
1¼ cups pin (cross-cut) oats, uncooked
1 bay leaf
1 small onion, chopped
1 small sage leaf, or to taste
   Salt and pepper, to taste
¼ cup flour
1 teaspoon salt
½ teaspoon paprika
¼ teaspoon pepper
   Butter or margarine, for cooking
   Butter and maple syrup

    Combine sausage and water in a medium saucepan. (Use a pan that is heavy and has a tight-fitting lid.) Mash sausage with a potato masher. Stir in oats; add bay leaf and chopped onion. Bring to a boil, then reduce heat so mixture simmers gently. Cook, covered, stirring every 10 or 15 minutes to make sure mixture doesn't stick. Use a straight-end spatula, pancake turner or similar device for stirring. After about 2 hours of cooking, add one small sage leaf, rubbed fine, and salt and pepper as needed. (This depends on the seasoning in the sausage.) Cook about 15 minutes longer.

Near end of cooking time, spoon off any fat that accumulates on surface. Then pour cooked mixture into a 9x5x3-inch loaf pan which has been rinsed with cold water. This will fill loaf pan about halfway. Cover and refrigerate.

To use, cut into ½-inch slices. Mix flour with salt, paprika and pepper. Coat slices with seasoned flour. Sauté slowly in butter in a skillet or on a griddle, until golden on both sides. Allow about 15 minutes cooking time. Serve with butter and maple syrup.

Note: This recipe was purposely given in small size. Double if you wish, keeping the proportions the same. Cooking time will be about the same.

Variation: *To make Scrapple,* proceed using same measurements except use cornmeal instead of pin oats. Stir cornmeal into cold liquid, rather than waiting for liquid to boil. Cook and stir until cornmeal thickens the mixture. (Cornmeal thickens more quickly than pin oats.) After the mixture has thickened, cover pan and set over a pan of boiling water to cook, stirring occasionally, about 1 hour.

Tasso is a smoked, highly seasoned strip of pork, usually taken from along the back of the hog. It's a product of the Cajun boucherie. Cajuns use it to season beans and such dishes as jambalaya, gumbo, etc. It takes well to long cooking.

WHITE BEANS AND TASSO
6 to 8 servings

1 pound dried white beans
  (navy or Great Northern)
½ to 1 pound tasso, cut in
  ½-inch cubes
2 large onions, chopped
2 cloves garlic, minced
1 tablespoon salt
1 teaspoon black pepper
  Cayenne, to taste

1 tablespoon Worcestershire
  sauce
¼ teaspoon dried oregano,
  crumbled
¼ teaspoon dried thyme,
  crumbled
1 bunch green onions,
  chopped
1 cup chopped fresh parsley
  Hot cooked rice

Cover beans with 2 quarts water and soak overnight. (Or, for quicker preparation, put beans in 2 quarts boiling water; remove from heat and allow to stand 1 hour.)

Bring beans and soaking water to a boil; reduce heat to low. Simmer 45 minutes. Add tasso and continue to simmer 1 hour. Add onions, garlic, salt, pepper, cayenne and Worcestershire sauce. Continue simmering for 1 more hour.

Remove from heat and allow to cool 30 minutes. Bring again to a boil. Add oregano, thyme, green onions and parsley. Reduce heat and simmer 30 minutes. Additional water can be added if needed (there should be a little "gravy"). Serve over rice.

Barbara Gibbs Ostmann

St. Louis Post-Dispatch / St. Louis, Missouri

About sixty miles south of St. Louis lies the charming, historic town of Ste. Genevieve. This picturesque town, on the banks of the Mississippi River, is Missouri's oldest existing town and the second-oldest town west of the Mississippi. It was settled by the French and still retains its French heritage. However, the German influence is stronger today than the French, and the culinary heritage of the town reflects the French, German and other cultural backgrounds.

Outstanding among the German dishes is a local specialty called leberknaefly, or liver dumplings. There are probably as many versions of this dish as there are cooks in Ste. Genevieve, but this one is representative.

LEBERKNAEFLY

6 to 10 servings

1 pound liver (calf, beef or pork)
½ cup ground pork
1 medium onion, finely chopped
3 cups all-purpose flour
3 eggs
1 tablespoon finely chopped parsley
½ teaspoon dried basil, or ½ teaspoon ground allspice
Salt and pepper, to taste
About 1 cup milk
Salted water
1 tablespoon fat

Grind liver; mix with ground pork and onion. Mix in flour, then add eggs, parsley, basil, salt and pepper. Add enough milk to make a stiff dough.

Transfer some of dough to a flat platter. Use a knife, dipped in hot water, to cut and drop tiny pieces of dough into boiling salted water to which fat has been added to keep dumplings from sticking together. When dumplings rise to the surface, they are ready to be skimmed off and drained.

Serve dumplings hot. Dumplings can be fried lightly in sausage drippings or served with a light gravy.

Note: The dough can be frozen for a short time.

Carol Hanson

The Post-Crescent / Appleton, Wisconsin

Cousin Jack Pasties are a treat my family seeks each time we return to Michigan's Upper Peninsula, where we lived for fifteen years. And we do return often!

We became well acquainted with pasties during those years—learning to eat them, steaming hot and covered with ketchup, just as the natives do. We carried them in our picnic basket, served them for lunch, savored them at casual parties.

This is a treasured recipe, given to me by a friend's mother who was considered by many to be one of the best pasty makers. She was Welsh, and a native of that area. Her recipe uses the traditional lard in the crust, with a sprinkle of suet topping the filling to ensure a moist interior.

COUSIN JACK PASTIES   *5 servings*

Dough:
- 3 cups all-purpose flour
- 1 tablespoon salt
- 1 cup lard
- 1 cup cold water

Filling:
- 3¾ cups cubed potatoes, divided
- 15 ounces flank steak, cubed, divided
- 5 ounces pork, cubed, divided
- 5 teaspoons suet, divided
- 5 tablespoons diced onion, divided
- Salt and pepper, to taste

For dough: Sift flour and salt into a mixing bowl; sift again. Cut in lard until mixture is the size of small peas; add cold water, a little at a time. Toss until mixture holds together, handling as little as possible. Cut into 5 portions. Roll each portion on a floured board until 9 inches across.

To fill: Place ¾ cup potatoes, 3 ounces flank steak, 1 ounce pork, 1 teaspoon suet, 1 tablespoon onion, salt and pepper on each portion of dough. Fold dough in half over filling, pinching edges to seal. Slit top. Repeat for other pasties. Place on a greased baking sheet. Bake in a 400°F oven 1 hour, or until nicely browned.

Gumbo is a classic dish in New Orleans. Just about every restaurant offers a version. This recipe uses ingredients that are available everywhere. Seafood gumbos are the most popular in New Orleans, but the ingredients are not so readily available in other parts of the country.

CHICKEN AND SAUSAGE GUMBO   *8 servings*

1 fryer (3 to 3½ pounds), cut up
½ cup bacon drippings or vegetable oil
½ cup all-purpose flour
2 onions, chopped
2 ribs celery, chopped
1 green pepper, chopped
6 to 8 cloves garlic, minced
1 to 1½ pounds smoked sausage, cut into ½-inch slices
2 quarts hot water or chicken stock
1 tablespoon salt
1 teaspoon black pepper
¼ teaspoon cayenne
½ cup chopped green onion tops
¼ cup finely chopped fresh parsley
2½ to 3 tablespoons gumbo filé (ground sassafras leaves)
Hot cooked rice

Brown chicken pieces in hot bacon drippings in a large, heavy pot. Remove chicken from pot and set aside. Make a roux by gradually adding flour to hot drippings, stirring constantly over medium heat until roux turns the color of a dirty copper penny, about 10 to 15 minutes. Do not let roux burn or gumbo will be ruined.

When roux reaches the right color, immediately stir in onion, celery, green pepper, garlic and sausage. Cook, stirring constantly, until vegetables are tender, or about 5 minutes. Add hot water, salt, pepper, cayenne and browned chicken pieces, stirring well to blend seasonings. Bring mixture to a boil; reduce heat and simmer 45 minutes to 1 hour, or until chicken is tender; stir occasionally. Stir in green onion and parsley; cook 5 minutes longer.

Remove gumbo from heat. Stir in filé and let stand 5 minutes to thicken. (Do not boil mixture after adding filé or it will become stringy.) Serve gumbo over rice with additional filé, if desired.

Note: Almost any kind of meat, poultry or seafood can be used in this recipe. You might want to try ham, shrimp, crab meat, oysters, pork, turkey or any game. For okra gumbo, add 2 cups fresh or frozen sliced okra with the sausage and omit filé.

Kitty Crider
Austin American-Statesman / Austin, Texas

The world's largest ranch, King Ranch, covers 900,000 acres in South Texas and extends into eight counties. The folks there don't eat beef at every meal; sometimes they have this casserole, which has become a favorite with homemakers and caterers because it's easy to extend. It has become the traditional Lone Star State standby for potluck suppers.

KING RANCH CHICKEN CASSEROLE   *8 to 10 servings*

  1 chicken (2½ to 3 pounds)
 12 corn tortillas, torn, or 16 taco shells, broken
  1 can (10¾ ounces) condensed cream of mushroom soup, undiluted
  1 can (10¾ ounces) condensed cream of chicken soup, undiluted
  1 large onion, chopped
  1 can (10 ounces) tomatoes with green chilies, undrained
  1 to 2 cups grated Cheddar cheese

Stew chicken in water in a large saucepot until tender. Reserve 1 cup chicken broth. Bone chicken, cutting meat into bite-size pieces.

Grease a 9x13x2-inch baking dish. Place torn tortillas or broken taco shells in bottom of dish. Layer chicken pieces on top. Combine soups, onion, tomatoes and reserved 1 cup chicken broth in saucepan; cook over medium heat until hot. Pour soup mixture over chicken. Top with grated cheese. Bake in a 350°F oven 50 to 60 minutes, or until bubbly hot.

Jean Thwaite
The Atlanta Journal-Constitution, / Altanta, Georgia

No one really seems to know the origin of this dish. Some say it was brought back from India to England by a British Navy officer. Others say it was a favorite in the English countryside and was originally Country Capon. The story Georgians like best is that it was created by an inventive Columbus cook for Franklin Delano Roosevelt when he was at the little White House in Warm Springs.

Still another version appears in "Georgia Heritage," published by the Colonial Dames. Mrs. Sewell Brumby of Athens writes that, some sixty-five years ago, her mother ordered a cookbook by Alexandre Fillipini, chef of Delmonico's for many years. Her mother changed this one dish radically, and it became a party favorite, taken all over the world by Army friends. Her mother's butler-chef ended up as chef at the White House and introduced it to Roosevelt. So take your pick.

Some versions call for using a hen, cooking it and pulling the meat off the bones. Others use cut-up fryers. The most recent ones use chicken breasts. The one constant seems to be that to be authentic, the recipe must call for currants and slivered toasted almonds. No raisins and pecans allowed.

CHICKEN COUNTRY CAPTAIN

12 servings

12 chicken breasts
   Flour and salt, for dredging chicken
2 generous tablespoons lard
2 onions, sliced fine
2 green peppers, sliced
2 cloves garlic, crushed
2 cans (16 ounces each) whole tomatoes, broken up
½ teaspoon white pepper
½ teaspoon dried thyme
1 to 2 teaspoons curry powder, or to taste
   Salt, to taste
3 heaping tablespoons currants soaked in 1 tablespoon white or
      red wine
   Cooked fluffy white rice (to serve 12)
¼ pound almonds, blanched, slivered and toasted
1 teaspoon chopped fresh parsley

Coat chicken pieces with flour and a little salt. Heat lard in a skillet. Fry chicken gently until brown. Remove chicken from skillet; put into a large casserole and keep warm.

Gently wilt onion and green pepper along with garlic in the same skillet. Add tomatoes, white pepper, thyme and curry powder; mix well. Check for salt, pepper and acidity. (Some canned tomatoes are more acidic than others and may need a little sugar.)

Pour the tomato sauce over chicken in casserole. Deglaze pan and add liquid to chicken. Cover tightly and cook on stovetop until chicken is very tender.

Put currants in a little wine and warm to plump. Place chicken breasts on a warmed platter. Make a ring of rice around chicken. Add currants to tomato sauce and pour sauce over rice and chicken. Scatter almonds over rice. Sprinkle with parsley.

Note: Curries are much better if made a day ahead; the seasonings blend into the meat much better. Rice can be cooked a day ahead, sealed in foil and reheated with the Country Captain.

Jann Malone

Richmond Times-Dispatch / Richmond, Virginia

I don't think I ever ate half a chicken in one sitting until I tasted the barbecued chicken at the 1982 Delmarva Chicken Festival—the chicken had a wonderful flavor that didn't stop at the skin but went all the way through the meat.

The secret is in the barbecue sauce—it turns out to be one that's been used on the Eastern Shore for some time. This version comes from Roy Beauchamp of Chesapeake Foods.

DELMARVA BARBECUED CHICKEN   *4 generous servings*

1 teaspoon salt
1 teaspoon pepper
2 teaspoons poultry seasoning
1 cup cider vinegar

½ cup vegetable oil
1 egg, well beaten
2 chickens, each split in half

Combine salt, pepper and poultry seasoning in a small bowl. Add vinegar, oil and egg; mix well.

When coals are ready, put chicken on the grill and baste with sauce. Keep mixing sauce as chicken cooks, because sauce tends to separate. Cook chicken slowly over medium coals 1½ to 2½ hours, or until juices run clear. Cooking time will depend on size of chicken. Baste chicken frequently with sauce, and turn chicken frequently.

Note: To serve 8, cut each half in two with poultry shears or a sharp knife.

Kit Snedaker

Los Angeles Herald Examiner / Los Angeles, California

The hottest fast-food item in Los Angeles is El Pollo Loco. Pass any of its nineteen locations anytime and watch lines of people waiting to order this Mexican-style char-broiled bird. Even the price is right. For under $6, you get a whole chicken, a container of fresh, spicy salsa and ten hot tortillas...enough for four people...but so good two can polish it off easily.

El Pollo Loco, or crazy chicken, was born eight years ago in Guasava, Mexico. Juan Francisco Ochao—Pancho to his friends—and his brother, Jaime, opened a roadside stand, broiling chicken for passersby. The first day, they sold fifty chickens and were on their way.

A year later, Jaime opened a restaurant specializing in the same fare, and it was equally successful. Today the family owns some ninety take-out eateries in Mexico.

In 1980, the Ochaos reasoned their chicken would be just as welcome to Mexicans elsewhere, and opened El Pollo Loco in the heart of the Hispanic community in Los Angeles.

El Pollo Loco's success spawned imitators. Now there's El Pollo Tonto (stupid chicken), Pollo Blanco (white chicken), Pollo de Oro (golden chicken), Pollo Gordo (fat chicken) and more.

El Pollo Loco's exact recipe is, of course, a secret, but rumor has it that the chicken is first marinated in something with fruit juices for twenty-four hours. When done, the skin is golden, and there are a few tinges of yellow on the meat, which means that it is either treated with food coloring (doubtful), turmeric or Mexican asafran, remotely related to saffron.

After experimenting with a good many "crazy chickens," Bess Greenstone, who writes regularly for the food section, came up with this recipe for "crazy chicken in your own kitchen."

EL POLLO LOCO DE TU COCINA

4 servings

3 quarts water
1 onion, coarsely chopped
2 carrots, coarsely
   chopped
3 to 4 sprigs fresh cilantro
2 teaspoons asafran or
   turmeric

1 tablespoon kosher salt
1 chicken (3½ to 4 pounds),
   quartered
Salsa
Hot tortillas

Combine water, onion, carrots, cilantro, asafran and salt in a large saucepot or Dutch oven. Bring to a boil and cook for 10 minutes. Add chicken. When liquids return to a boil, cook for 5 minutes. Turn off the heat and cover pot. Allow chicken to cool in the broth.

Remove chicken to a platter. Reduce broth to half by rapid boiling. Place chicken on grill over hot coals and cook until done. Baste with broth and turn frequently. Serve with salsa and tortillas.

Marge Hanley

Indianapolis News / Indianapolis, Indiana

The Iron Skillet restaurant in Indianapolis is part of the city's culinary heritage. It's known for its Hoosier fried chicken dinners, complete with whipped potatoes, cream gravy, green beans seasoned with ham and onion, and buttered corn.

THE IRON SKILLET'S HOOSIER FRIED CHICKEN

3 to 4 servings per chicken

Chicken fryers (2½ to 3 pounds each)
Salt

All-purpose flour
Lard for frying

Clean, cut and salt chicken pieces the day before frying. Cover and refrigerate.

When ready to fry, coat pieces with flour, shaking off excess. Heat lard, about 1 inch deep in large skillet. Add chicken pieces to hot lard, being sure chicken is not added too quickly, as it may reduce lard temperature. Turn chicken and brown on both sides. Reduce heat so lard is about 275°F. Continue frying and turning chicken pieces until crisp and well done, about 25 to 35 minutes, depending upon size of pieces. Drain and serve immediately.

Mary Frances Phillips

San Jose Mercury News / San Jose, California

This is healthy California cooking at its finest. A good friend, Jim, showed me how to make this dish. Complete the California meal with rice pilaf (rice, chicken stock and sautéed onion), fresh zucchini or string beans, and a platter of fresh strawberries, cantaloupe slices and kiwi halves.

CALIFORNIA BAKED CHICKEN

2 to 4 servings

1 frying chicken (3 to 3½ pounds)
3 to 5 large cloves garlic

Melted butter for basting
Herbs (optional)

Rinse and dry chicken, removing gizzard, heart, etc. Place chicken in single-chicken-size granite roaster. Insert garlic cloves in cavity; tie legs together with butcher's string. Baste with melted butter. Sprinkle with herbs, if desired. Cover with lid. Bake in a 500°F (this is correct) oven for 30 minutes. Reduce temperature to 350°F and bake 1 hour more.

Place chicken on a platter, cut down through breast with a case knife and remove bones.

Ann Criswell

Houston Chronicle / Houston, Texas

Chicken-Fried Steak is one of the most traditional Texas foods, linked to both our Old West and our Southern heritage. To prepare them for the cowboys, range cooks would tenderize tough beefsteaks with a cleaver, season them with salt and pepper, dust them with flour and fry them in sizzling fat.

In West Texas, Chicken-Fried Steak is typically served with a skillet gravy made from drippings and water, with a little flour for thickening. In East Texas and some other areas, a batter like fried chicken batter is used, and the steaks are served with cream gravy made from pan drippings or butter, flour and milk. Don't skimp on the gravy!

TEXAS CHICKEN-FRIED STEAK

4 to 6 servings

2 pounds round steak	1 teaspoon salt
2 eggs	¼ teaspoon pepper
½ cup milk	Vegetable oil for frying
1 cup all-purpose flour	Cream Gravy (recipe follows)

Cut steak in serving pieces and pound flat with a tenderizer mallet. Beat eggs with milk. Mix flour with salt and pepper. Dip steak in egg mixture, then in seasoned flour. Fry in ½ inch of hot oil in a large skillet until brown on both sides. Serve with gravy.

CREAM GRAVY

1 cup

1 tablespoon butter or drippings	1 cup milk or half-and-half, warmed
1 to 2 tablespoons all-purpose flour	Salt and pepper

If using butter, melt in skillet. Stir in flour. Remove from heat; whisk in milk. Return to heat and stir until thickened. Season to taste with salt and pepper. (I like a healthy sprinkling of pepper.)

Carol Brock

Daily News / New York, New York

Not only is New York the nation's melting pot; it is its cooking pot as well, providing recipes for menus across the land. Many dishes enjoy a short period of popularity and then fade away. But some outlive the fabled restaurants and hotels that made them famous, adding to New York's reputation as a cradle of culinary invention.

The legacy of Delmonico's is a case in point. Although the restaurant died along with the age of opulence that spawned it, many of its dishes are still served throughout America. Delmonico's was one of several earlier-day eateries that helped to establish New York's way with steak, and the Delmonico Steak is, obviously, named for the restaurant.

DELMONICO STEAK   *2 servings*

 2 Delmonico steaks (about 1¼ pounds each), cut from rib eye
     roast
   Salt
   Melted butter or olive oil

Maître d'Hotel Butter:
 4 tablespoons butter, softened
 1 tablespoon minced parsley
¼ teaspoon salt
   Pepper
½ teaspoon lemon juice

Start heating the broiler 10 minutes ahead of time. Sprinkle steak with salt and brush with melted butter. For a 1½-inch thick steak, broil 9 minutes per side for rare, 10 minutes for medium, 12 to 13 minutes for well done.

For Maître d'Hotel Butter: While steak is broiling, blend softened butter with parsley, salt, a speck of pepper and lemon juice. Serve butter in individual containers alongside steaks.

Fajitas (fah-heet-us), marinated skirt steak cut into pieces and served in a warm flour tortilla, is a popular specialty in northern Mexico that's catching on in Texas and the Southwest like wildfire.

The meat is usually labeled skirt steak in the supermarket and is a thin, flat piece of beef somewhat resembling flank steak. It is actually a supportive organ that comes from the inside of the rib cage.

The meat is marinated several hours or overnight, then drained and quickly grilled over coals, chopped into small pieces, then rolled up and served in a warm flour tortilla. Usually a variety of sauces accompanies fajitas—Guacamole, Salsa Verde (a mild green chili sauce), Salsa Roja (a hotter red sauce) or Salsa Cruda, a mixture of fresh chopped tomatoes, white onion, a little cilantro (fresh coriander) and a dash of salt and pepper (mashed or chopped jalapeño peppers are optional).

Like brisket, skirt steak has a layer of fat that should be trimmed. Any membrane also should be peeled off so the meat won't be too chewy. The steak should be thin; if it is more than ¾-inch thick at the thickest portion, cut it in half lengthwise so that it will cook quickly. The rule for cooking is hot fire, short cooking time.

Various marinades are used. Some cooks just use bottled barbecue sauce, but a mixture of beer, a little oil, garlic and chopped vegetables is more typical. This marinade comes from one of our photographers, Carlos Antonio Rios.

FAJITAS
1 quart marinade

4 cups soy sauce (the heavy dark imported kind is too strong)
1 cup packed light brown sugar
1 teaspoon garlic powder
1 teaspoon onion powder
8 tablespoons fresh lemon juice
4 teaspoons ground ginger
1 skirt steak (about ¾-inch thickness) for every 3 persons
Warm flour tortillas

Combine soy sauce, brown sugar, garlic powder, onion powder, lemon juice and ginger in a jar; shake to mix well and dissolve sugar. Let marinade stand in sealed jar overnight. Pour marinade over beef and let marinate 2 hours or overnight in refrigerator in sealed container.

Remove fajitas from marinade and grill over very hot coals a short time, about 10 minutes per steak if meat is ¾-inch thick. Brush meat with marinade two or three times while cooking.

Refrigerate extra marinade in tightly sealed jar for future use.

Chop meat with a cleaver and wrap in warm flour tortillas to serve.

Texas pit barbecue requires three essential ingredients: a good solid (5- to 10-pound) piece of beef, brisket by choice, well marbled with fat; a slow-burning or smoldering fire using mesquite or oak; and a "pit." The pit is made either from stone or from a 55-gallon drum. The meat is not grilled over the coals, but rather smoked for four to eight hours in the draft of the hot fumes and smoke from the fire.

Some people say that good barbecue can only be achieved south of the Red River. That's where mesquite and live oak are most plentiful; these produce the slow heat and savory smoke flavor that make first-rate barbecue.

Everyone has his own special barbecue sauce for marinating, basting and pouring over the sliced meat. There is a basic recipe to which your own "secret" ingredients can be added.

The use of the sauce, however it is prepared, varies from person to person and locale to locale. It may be used to marinate the beef overnight, as a baster during the cooking process, and/or as a gravy served with the meat.

Slow cooking away from direct heat will produce delicious barbecue beef that is well done through and through, and soft, tender and juicy.

Barbecue is traditionally eaten with potato salad, onions, pickles and a slice of bread or saltine crackers.

BASIC BARBECUE SAUCE
FOR TEXAS PIT BARBECUE

¾ to 1 cup

1 medium onion, chopped
1 clove garlic, minced
2 tablespoons butter or
    margarine
½ cup ketchup
¼ cup water
2 tablespoons vinegar

1 tablespoon light brown sugar
1 teaspoon prepared mustard
    Salt and pepper, to taste
½ teaspoon hot pepper sauce
    (optional)
1 lemon or orange, sliced
    (optional)

Cook onion and garlic in butter in a medium saucepan until tender. Add ketchup, water, vinegar, brown sugar, mustard, salt, pepper and hot pepper sauce. Bring to a boil. Remove from heat and let stand for flavors to mingle.

A sliced lemon or orange can be added, or a bit of the juice of either.

Note: "Secret" ingredients include beer, wine, bourbon, bay leaves, chili powder, tomatoes, vegetable oil or fat.

Billie Bledsoe

San Antonio Express-News / San Antonio, Texas

This is one of the most famous barbecue recipes in Texas—and the origin, of course, is obvious. President Lyndon B. Johnson gets all the credit for this one.

LBJ BARBECUE SAUCE
2½ cups

1 cup ketchup
½ cup cider vinegar
1 teaspoon granulated sugar
1 teaspoon chili powder
½ teaspoon salt
1½ cups water
3 ribs celery, chopped
3 bay leaves

1 clove garlic, minced
2 tablespoons chopped onion
4 tablespoons Worcestershire
   sauce
1 teaspoon paprika
   Dash black pepper
4 tablespoons butter

Combine ketchup, vinegar, sugar, chili powder, salt, water, celery, bay leaves, garlic, onion, Worcestershire sauce, paprika, pepper and butter in a medium saucepan. Bring mixture to a boil. Simmer 15 minutes. Remove from heat and strain.

This is a modern adaption of an old Chickasaw Indian recipe which was originally made with venison.

CHICKASAW BAKED STEAK   *6 servings*

2 pounds rump steak (½-inch thickness), cut in 6 pieces, pounded
   Salt and pepper, to taste
   All-purpose flour, for dredging
   Butter or vegetable oil, for frying
1 large onion, chopped fine
1 large green pepper, chopped
½ cup chopped celery
½ cup sherry
½ cup tomato sauce or tomato juice
½ teaspoon paprika
1 cup water

Season steak with salt and pepper. Dip pieces in flour and fry in butter or oil for 1 minute on each side. Transfer steaks to a pan suitable for baking.

Sauté onion, green pepper and celery in same skillet. Add sherry, tomato sauce, paprika and water. Pour over steaks in baking dish. Bake, uncovered, in a 375°F oven 30 minutes. Turn steaks over and bake another 30 minutes.

This isn't a World Championship chili recipe. It would have to be doctored to reach those gastronomic heights. But it's real. It is based on the formula used by famed chuck wagon cook Richard Bolt from the 175,000-acre 4-Sixes Ranch in West Texas, one of the largest ranches to outfit a chuck wagon.

TEXAS CHUCK WAGON CHILI   *6 to 8 servings*

   3 pounds beef chuck roast, cut into small stew-size chunks
        (including fat)
   6 tablespoons chili powder
   3 tablespoons ground oregano
   6 cloves garlic, minced
   3 tablespoons ground cumin (cominos)
   1 tablespoon cayenne (less if you don't like it really hot)
1½ to 2 quarts water
   ⅓ cup masa harina or cornmeal

   Using some of the fat, render fat for browning rest of meat. Brown meat in a cast-iron Dutch oven. Add chili powder, oregano, garlic, cumin and cayenne. Stir to coat meat. Add water and stir. Bring liquid to a boil and simmer, covered, for 1 to 1½ hours. Make a thick paste of masa or cornmeal and add to chili stew. Stir to prevent lumping. Remove lid and simmer 30 to 45 minutes longer (more if you like) to thicken and reduce stew to desired consistency.

Note: You may need to tone down the seasonings to suit more tender, non-Texas palates. An Ohio food editor tamed it down to 3 tablespoons chili powder, 2 teaspoons ground cumin, 1½ teaspoons ground oregano and 1 teaspoon cayenne, to start.

San Antonio is famous for its annual Fiesta which features the many ethnic recipes which are part of the city's culture. Literally hundreds of thousands of these anticuchos are sold every year.

ANTICUCHOS

2 to 4 servings

¾ cup red wine vinegar
2¼ cups water
2 to 3 serrano peppers
Salt
Whole black peppercorns
½ to 1 teaspoon garlic salt, or
   2 to 3 cloves garlic

Big pinch dried oregano
Big pinch ground cumin
   (cominos)
1 to 2 pounds cubed meat
   (beef or pork)
Bacon grease

Put vinegar, water, peppers, salt, peppercorns, garlic salt, oregano and cumin in container of an electric blender; blend well. Pour over cubed meat in a nonmetallic bowl; marinade should cover meat. Let marinate in refrigerator at least several hours; overnight is preferable.

Remove cubes of meat from marinade, saving marinade. Skewer meat. Add bacon grease to reserved marinade and use as a basting sauce. Cook meat over hot coals until done. (The bacon grease adds additional flavor and makes the meat smoke during cooking.)

Chili Relleno Casserole is a good example of Southern California cooking. It is good with char-broiled steak, or alone with Spanish rice and a salad.

CHILI RELLENO CASSEROLE

6 servings

6 green chilies (fresh, roasted and peeled; or canned)
6 ounces Monterey Jack cheese, cut in strips
4 eggs
⅓ cup milk
½ cup all-purpose flour
½ teaspoon baking powder

1 cup shredded longhorn cheese
1 can (8 ounces) tomato sauce, seasoned with herbs of choice
Pitted ripe olives, chopped, for garnish

Stuff chilies with Monterey Jack cheese strips (or use a mixture of Monterey Jack and longhorn, if preferred). Arrange stuffed chilies side by side in a greased shallow baking dish.

Beat eggs with an electric mixer until thick and foamy. Add milk, flour and baking powder. Beat until as smooth as possible (batter will be a little lumpy). Pour batter over chilies, making sure that all the chilies are moist. Sprinkle with longhorn cheese.

Bake, uncovered, in a 375°F oven 25 minutes, or until casserole is puffed and appears set. Just before casserole is ready, heat seasoned tomato sauce to serve in a gravy boat. Garnish hot casserole with chopped olives.

Note: This can be assembled ahead of time and refrigerated. When ready to serve, bake in a 375°F oven 35 minutes.

For typical California fare, serve this hot tamale pie with a green salad, sourdough bread or baking powder biscuits, red wine and a fresh fruit platter.

HOT TAMALE PIE

6 to 8 servings

Cornmeal Crust:
1 cup yellow cornmeal
1 cup water
2 cups boiling water
1 teaspoon salt
2 tablespoons butter or margarine

Filling:
1 pound lean ground beef
1 large onion, minced
2 tablespoons vegetable oil
2 tablespoons all-purpose flour

2 cans (8 ounces each) tomato sauce
⅓ cup Burgundy or claret wine
2 teaspoons chili powder, or more, to taste
½ teaspoon cumin seeds (optional)
Salt, garlic salt and pepper, to taste
1 cup whole ripe pitted black olives
1 can (16 ounces) whole kernel corn, drained
½ cup grated natural Cheddar cheese

For crust: Combine cornmeal with 1 cup water in top of a double boiler; mix until smooth. Gradually stir in 2 cups boiling water; add salt. Stir constantly over direct heat until mixture thickens. Add butter. Cover and cook over boiling water for 20 minutes, stirring occasionally. Line a well-greased 2-quart baking dish with mixture, smoothing it evenly over surface of dish with your fingers or the back of a spoon. This is easier to do when mixture is slightly cool. Next, prepare filling.

For filling: Sauté beef and onion in oil until meat is no longer red, stirring with a fork so meat is broken into small bits. Blend in flour; add tomato sauce and wine. Cook, stirring constantly, until mixture boils and thickens. Simmer 5 minutes or so. Add chili powder, cumin seed, salt, garlic salt, pepper, olives and corn.

Pour filling into cornmeal crust. Sprinkle with grated cheese. Bake in a 350°F oven 45 minutes.

Many recipes for Cincinnati Chili are called Empress Chili. Empress is a local chili parlor chain begun by a Greek family. That chain, and its competitors, add cinnamon and make the beef fine textured by simmering it in water. The real recipe is secret, so many versions float around.

In a Cincinnati chili parlor, you must know the lingo. Chili is always ladled over spaghetti, with shredded cheese on top, and oyster crackers on the side. That's "three-way chili." "Four-way chili" has chopped onion. "Five-way chili" has kidney beans, too.

CINCINNATI CHILI

6 servings (1½ quarts)

2 pounds ground beef
2 medium onions, chopped
1 quart water
1 can (16 ounces) tomatoes
1½ teaspoons vinegar
1 teaspoon Worcestershire sauce
1 tablespoon chili powder
2 teaspoons ground cumin (cominos)
1½ teaspoons ground allspice
1½ teaspoons salt
1 teaspoon cayenne

1 teaspoon ground cinnamon
½ teaspoon garlic powder
2 bay leaves
6 servings hot, cooked spaghetti
1½ cups shredded Cheddar cheese
1 carton (11 or 12 ounces) oyster crackers
1 cup chopped onion (optional)
1 can (16 ounces) kidney beans, heated (optional)

Combine ground beef, onions and water in a saucepan. Simmer until beef turns brown. Add tomatoes with liquid, vinegar, Worcestershire sauce, chili powder, cumin, allspice, salt, cayenne, cinnamon, garlic powder and bay leaves. Cover; simmer 3 hours.

The fat will float. If there is time, chill chili and lift off fat layer. Or spoon off fat.

To serve basic "three-way chili," serve chili on spaghetti and top with cheese. Pass oyster crackers. For "four-way chili," add chopped onion. For "five-way chili," spoon heated kidney beans on top.

Mary Alice Powell
The Blade / Toledo, Ohio

For years, downtown Toledo boasted a chili parlor, really a greasy spoon, but everyone raved about the Chili Mac. We came up with this recipe the night a pressman hosted a former chili-parlor cook to an over-consumption of beer and he began to utter the secret ingredients.

CHILI MAC, TOLEDO STYLE   8 servings

1 tablespoon solid shortening
1¼ cups cubed or ground suet
1¼ cups water, divided
2¼ pounds coarse ground beef, divided
1 onion (about 2¼ inches), chopped
4 or 5 cloves garlic, finely chopped
3½ teaspoons hot chili powder
1 teaspoon crushed dried red peppers
¾ teaspoon cumin seeds

¼ teaspoon black pepper
1 teaspoon ground sage
¼ teaspoon cayenne
1 teaspoon salt
½ teaspoon monosodium glutamate (MSG)
Cooked pinto beans (no chili seasoning)
Cooked spaghetti
Grated Parmesan cheese
Additional crushed dried red peppers (optional)

Place shortening, suet, small amount of water (about ¼ cup) and a little of the ground beef in a large pan. Cover and cook on medium heat until suet softens. Then add remaining beef and brown. Add onion, garlic, the remaining water, chili powder, dried peppers, cumin seed, black pepper, sage, cayenne, salt and MSG. Simmer on low heat, uncovered, until sauce becomes orange and oily and no longer watery, about 1 hour. Sauce must be stirred frequently.

To serve, nestle cooked beans in cooked spaghetti and spoon meat sauce over all. Sprinkle generously with Parmesan cheese. If desired, serve with additional crushed dried red peppers.

Billie Bledsoe

San Antonio Express-News / San Antonio, Texas

Like the Alamo, this is a feature of Texas EVERYONE knows. What is more, every Texan has THE best recipe for it, and probably one or two ancestors who knew the guy who invented it. It is a strictly Texan dish; you won't find it south of the border.

Chili meat is most often mature, muscular beef (neck or shoulder); sometimes goat, venison or rabbit. The important thing is that it should be solid enough to withstand long cooking. The meat is usually in small cubes, but there are those who use it chopped, shredded and even ground. Some add onions; some add tomato; any of the chili peppers is eligible, and other spices—from bay leaf to paprika—may be added. It may be served with or without beans. These variations make each new "bowl of red" an adventure.

Try this version for a start.

CHILI CON CARNE
8 to 10 servings

3 pounds cubed beef
2 tablespoons vegetable oil or lard, for cooking
4 cups water
⅓ teaspoon cayenne
2 tablespoons ground cumin (cominos)

5 tablespoons chili powder
2 teaspoons salt
4 cloves garlic, pressed
3 teaspoons dried oregano
2 tablespoons paprika
1 can (6 ounces) tomato paste
Sugar, to taste

Cook meat in oil in a large skillet or Dutch oven until gray in color. Add water and simmer for 30 minutes. Add cayenne, cumin, chili powder, salt, garlic, oregano, paprika and tomato paste. Simmer at least 2 hours, until meat is tender. A pinch of sugar helps to bind the flavors and mellow them. (If mixture seems too thin, pour off some and mix with flour to thicken, then return to pot and stir.)

Serve steaming hot in a bowl, with minced onion on top, if you like, and crackers or tortillas.

Chicago Tribune / Chicago, Illinois

The following two pizzas are unique to Chicago. The first is the original deep-dish Chicago pizza, with a cornmeal-based crust and sausage and cheese filling baked in a two-inch deep pizza pan.

The second pizza is fast gaining Chicago converts over the deep-dish. It is the stuffed pizza—the filling is lodged between two layers of dough and then topped with a fresh tomato sauce.

CHICAGO DEEP-DISH PIZZA

6 servings

Crust:
  1 cup water
  ¼ cup solid shortening
  1½ tablespoons granulated
    sugar
  2¼ teaspoons salt
  1½ packages active dry yeast
  ½ cup lukewarm water
  ¾ cup yellow cornmeal
  3 to 3½ cups all-purpose
    flour
  Vegetable oil
Filling:
  1 can (28 ounces) Italian-style
    tomatoes
  1 small onion, chopped

  1 small green pepper,
    chopped
  1 clove garlic, minced
  ¾ teaspoon dried oregano
  ½ teaspoon fennel seeds
  ½ teaspoon salt
  ¼ teaspoon pepper
  2 tablespoons vegetable oil
  1 can (4 ounces) sliced
    mushrooms, drained
  1 pound mild Italian sausage
  1 package (10 ounces)
    mozzarella cheese, thinly
    sliced
  ½ cup grated Parmesan
    cheese

For crust: Heat 1 cup water, shortening, sugar and salt until shortening melts; cool to lukewarm. Soften yeast in ½ cup lukewarm water. Combine yeast and shortening mixtures in a large bowl. Add cornmeal. Add 2 cups of the flour; beat well. Stir in enough additional flour to make a soft dough. Turn onto a lightly floured board; knead until smooth and elastic, working in more flour as needed. Brush a round, 12-inch pizza pan (at least 2 inches deep) with oil. Press dough evenly over bottom and up sides of pan. Bake in a preheated 425°F oven 5 minutes.

For filling: Drain tomatoes in colander; chop tomatoes and return to colander; set aside to drain. Sauté onion, green pepper, garlic, oregano, fennel seeds, salt and pepper in oil until onion and green pepper are tender. Stir in well-drained tomatoes and mushrooms; cook lightly, then remove from heat.

Remove sausage from casing; crumble into pizza crust (sausage need not be cooked beforehand). Arrange mozzarella slices over sausage. Top with tomato mixture; sprinkle with Parmesan cheese. Bake in a 425°F oven 45 minutes, or until crust is golden brown. Let stand 5 minutes before serving.

CHICAGO STUFFED SPINACH PIZZA

6 servings

Dough:
1 tablespoon granulated
  sugar
2 packages active dry yeast
2 cups very warm water
  (105°F to 115°F)
⅓ cup vegetable oil
4 to 6 cups all-purpose flour

Sauce:
2 tablespoons olive oil
1 clove garlic, minced
1 can (28 ounces) crushed
  tomatoes with added
  puree
2 teaspoons dried oregano
1½ teaspoons dried basil
½ teaspoon salt
½ teaspoon freshly ground
  pepper

Filling:
3 packages (10 ounces each)
  frozen chopped spinach,
  thawed, well drained
2½ cups shredded mozzarella
  cheese
½ cup freshly grated
  Parmesan cheese
½ cup freshly grated Romano
  cheese
¼ teaspoon salt
¼ teaspoon freshly ground
  black pepper
1 teaspoon dried basil
2 cloves garlic, minced
2 tablespoons olive oil
2 cups sliced mushrooms
  (optional)

For dough: Dissolve sugar and yeast in water in a large bowl; let stand until bubbly. Stir in oil. Stir in 4 cups of the flour until smooth; stir in remaining flour as needed until stiff dough forms. Knead on lightly floured surface until smooth and elastic. Put in greased bowl; turn to coat top. Let rise, covered, in a warm place for 1 hour, or until double in bulk.

For sauce: Heat olive oil in a large saucepan. Add garlic; sauté 2 minutes. Stir in tomatoes, oregano, basil, salt and pepper. Simmer 30 minutes, or until very thick.

For filling: Mix spinach, mozzarella, Parmesan, Romano, salt, pepper, basil, garlic, olive oil and mushrooms in a large bowl.

Punch dough down. Let rest 10 minutes. Roll two-thirds of dough into a 16-inch circle. Fit into 12-inch diameter, deep-dish pizza pan; let sides of dough overhang.

Put spinach filling into center of dough; smooth evenly over surface. Roll remaining one-third of dough on lightly floured surface to a 12-inch circle. Put over filling; crimp edges; cut excess dough at edges so dough is level with top crust. Pour tomato sauce over dough to cover. Bake in a preheated 450°F oven 30 to 40 minutes, or until dough is golden.

Jane Baker
The Phoenix Gazette / Phoenix, Arizona

The Southwest has many foods that are dubbed "Mexican" when they really are American-Mexican creations. One example is chimichangas (pronounced chee-mee-chan-gas). Arizonans like to think they are their own invention, but you now can find them on many Mexican restaurant menus in the United States. The Mexicans, of course, have never heard of "chimis."

A chimichanga is a flour tortilla filled with a meat or bean mixture and deep-fried. The tortillas become flaky, like pastry dough, when they are fried.

CHIMICHANGAS

6 servings
(12 chimichangas)

2½ cups Shredded Beef Filling (recipe follows)
12 flour tortillas (7 inches in diameter)
    Vegetable oil or solid shortening, for frying

Shredded lettuce
1½ cups shredded Cheddar cheese
Dairy sour cream or guacamole (optional)

Spoon 3 tablespoons meat filling down the center of 1 tortilla. Fold sides of tortilla over filling and roll it up. Secure with a toothpick, if necessary. Assemble only 2 or 3 at a time, because the tortilla will absorb liquid from the sauce.

Deep-fry in hot oil (about 350°F) in a deep-fryer 1 to 2 minutes, or until golden brown. Lift from fat with a slotted spoon. Drain well. Keep in a warm oven and finish cooking the rest.

Serve on a bed of shredded lettuce; top with cheese and, if desired, sour cream or guacamole.

SHREDDED BEEF FILLING

2½ cups

1 medium onion, chopped
1½ tablespoons vegetable oil
2 cups finely chopped or shredded cooked lean beef (leftovers from a pot roast are good)

1 can (4 ounces) chopped green chilies
1 teaspoon ground cumin (optional)
1 cup canned or homemade enchilada sauce

Sauté onion in hot oil in a skillet. Blend in beef, chilies, cumin and enchilada sauce. Simmer 10 minutes, stirring occasionally. Use to fill Chimichangas.

Note: This beef filling also can be used for tacos, enchiladas or tamales.

SMOTHERED BURRITOS

Smothered Burritos are unique to Denver, at least as far as visiting Mexican food experts tell us. A Smothered Burrito is a seasoned beef or beef and bean burrito covered with a green or red chili gravy. Sam Arnold, local expert on chilies, gave me his favorite recipe.

Spread warm refried beans on a flour tortilla. Sprinkle with chicharonnes (you can substitute crisp bacon bits), chopped green onions and green chili gravy (recipe follows). (Sam likes his chili gravy inside the burrito.) Roll up tortilla, enclosing filling. Cook in a microwave oven or under a broiler to warm through.

If you want the burrito smothered, just hold the gravy until after you have rolled up the tortilla, then liberally cover burrito with gravy.

Make green chili gravy by adding pureed, peeled and roasted Anaheim chilies to a roux of flour and butter. Season with oregano and salt to taste. Use to make burrito described above.

Serve Smothered Burritos garnished with shredded lettuce, shredded cheese and chopped tomato.

Note: Some chili-fanciers add diced pork to the chili gravy for a more filling meal.

BREAKFAST BURRITOS

Sam also has a favorite recipe for Breakfast Burritos from Santa Fe, New Mexico.

Spread crisp hashed brown potatoes and 3 to 4 pieces of crisp bacon, crumbled, on a flour tortilla. Roll up. Top with grated Monterey Jack cheese and green or red chili puree. If desired, add a fried egg sunny-side up. Put in the oven long enough to melt cheese. Serve immediately.

TOASTED CHILIES AND CHEESE

This is another Sante Fe breakfast item from Sam.

Toast a green chili under the broiler until skin is puffed and well browned. Rotate chili to brown (char) all sides. Peel, but do not seed. Put chili on a plate and top with a pat of butter and a slice of Havarti cheese. Cook in a microwave oven or under a broiler until cheese melts. Serve with crisp French bread and, if desired, scrambled eggs.

Jane Baker

The Phoenix Gazette / Phoenix, Arizona

Admittedly, the Tuba City (Arizona) Truck Stop Cafe is not on the way to anywhere. It's north of Flagstaff, on the western edge of the Navajo nation. But this cafe makes the best Navajo Tacos. Many native Americans are well known for their fry bread—particularly the Navajos. This taco, which uses fry bread as a base, is unusual—and very tasty. If your journeys don't take you to Tuba City, here's my rendition of the cafe's recipe.

NAVAJO TACOS   *6 large servings*

6 dinner-plate-size pieces fry bread (recipe follows)

3 cups chili with beans (homemade or canned), heated

1 cup chopped onion

1½ cups chopped fresh tomatoes

3 large green chilies, seeded, deveined and chopped

2 cups shredded lettuce

1½ cups grated Cheddar cheese

Salsa or hot pepper sauce (optional)

Place each warm fry bread on a large plate. For each taco, layer a portion of warm chili, onion, tomato, chilies and lettuce on fry bread. Top with a portion of cheese. Serve immediately with salsa or hot pepper sauce, if desired.

NAVAJO FRY BREAD

4 cups all-purpose flour
1 tablespoon baking powder
1 teaspoon salt
2 tablespoons nonfat dry milk
    powder

1¼ to 1½ cups warm water
1 to 2 cups solid shortening
    or lard, for frying

Combine flour, baking powder, salt and dry milk powder in a large mixing bowl. Gradually stir in warm water. Mix until dough forms a ball and comes clean from edge of bowl. You may need to add a little additional water.

Knead dough with your hands until well mixed and dough is elastic. Divide dough into 6 large pieces and roll into balls. Using palms of your hands, pat out dough into circles that are about ½-inch thick.

Melt shortening in a large skillet. You will need about ¾ inch of melted fat. Heat to 500°F. Slip a rounded, flat piece of dough into the hot fat—it will start to rise to the top. When the underside is brown, turn over and brown the other side. Drain on paper towels. Repeat with remaining dough. Use to make Navajo Tacos.

Note: If you just want to make fry bread—it's a great snack sprinkled with confectioners sugar or drizzled with honey—divide dough into small portions to make 2-inch balls. This recipe will make 8 to 10 smaller portions.

Marilynn Marter
The Philadelphia Inquirer / Philadelphia, Pennsylvania

PHILADELPHIA CHEESE-STEAK

"Philadelphia's greatest gifts to our society are as follows:
"Seventeenth Century: Religious freedom
"Eighteenth Century: Political independence
"Nineteenth Century: Culture
"Twentieth Century: The cheese-steak."

Thus began an ode to the Philadelphia Cheese-Steak by Bill Collins, a staff writer. According to loyal cheese-steak fans, the sandwich, in all its greasy glory, is the greatest gastronomical advance since cooking oil.

Begun more than fifty years ago at a small sandwich stand in South Philadelphia, the basic cheese-steak is composed of thinly sliced beef (usually rib eye or eye of round), mild American cheese (or gooey Cheez Whiz) and Italian bread (either a torpedo-shaped roll or a half of a long, thin loaf). The meat is fried on a griddle with oil. If real cheese is used, it is melted over the nearly done meat. The meat is placed on the bread, then topped with fried onion slivers and sauce—sweet, spicy or bland (or just plain ketchup). Sometimes a cheese-steak is topped with mustard, fried mushroom slices, or sweet or hot peppers.

For the sake of outsiders, here is an explanation of cheese-steakese: "One with" is a cheese-steak with fried onions. "One cheese" is a plain cheese-steak. "One" is a steak sandwich without adornment.

There is even an art to eating a cheese-steak. One must execute a perfect cheese-steak bend from the waist to avoid spilling food on one's clothes.

Legend has it that this culinary delicacy began back in 1930 or 1932. Business was so bad at Pat Olivieri's South Philadelphia hot dog stand that when a cab driver saw Pat preparing some grilled beef on a roll for dinner for himself, the cabbie suggested that the resulting concoction would sell better than Pat's hot dogs. Soon thereafter, Pat perfected the first cheese-steak. Because the invention wasn't patented, the question of who actually made the first cheese-steak may never be answered. But to Philadelphians, "Pat's King of Steaks" at Ninth and Passyunk is the birthplace of the city's special sandwich. Numerous other eateries now offer the same treat, or various versions thereof.

The Hot Brown takes its name from the hotel in whose kitchen it originated. The Brown Hotel opened in 1923, and it is believed that the first Hot Brown was served shortly thereafter. Although the Brown Hotel is now closed, its name lives on in its sandwich, which is served in restaurants all around the city.

As the story goes, a chef at the Brown Hotel in the 1920s came up with an idea to use leftover turkey. He put the turkey on toast points and covered it with a cheese sauce. It was dubbed a Hot Brown. Today, there are many versions of the recipe. This one is the Brown's original, from the files of The Courier-Journal's *late food editor, Cissy Gregg.*

LOUISVILLE HOT BROWN   *4 servings*

4 tablespoons butter
1 small onion, chopped
4 tablespoons all-purpose flour
2 cups milk
½ teaspoon salt
¼ teaspoon white pepper
¼ cup shredded Cheddar
    cheese

¼ cup grated Parmesan cheese
8 slices trimmed toast
Cooked chicken or turkey
    breast, sliced
Crisp-fried bacon, crumbled
Mushroom slices, sautéed

Melt butter in a saucepan. Sauté onion in butter until transparent. Add flour; mix well. Stir in milk, salt and pepper; whisk until smooth. Cook over medium heat until sauce thickens, stirring occasionally. Add Cheddar cheese and Parmesan cheese; continue heating until cheeses are melted and blended with sauce. Remove sauce from heat.

Put 1 slice of toast in each of four oven-proof individual serving dishes. Top each piece of toast with slices of chicken or turkey. Cut remaining toast slices diagonally and place 2 triangles alongside each sandwich. Ladle cheese sauce equally over all four sandwiches. Place dishes under broiler until sauce begins to bubble, about 2 minutes. Garnish with crumbled bacon and sautéed mushroom slices. Serve immediately.

Diane Wiggins

St. Louis Globe-Democrat / St. Louis, Missouri

At a recent professional meeting, talk turned, as always, to food. When the subject of local specialties came up, we were introduced to a new one, courtesy of Bob Gonko of the State Journal-Register *in Springfield, Illinois.*

THE SPRINGFIELD HORSESHOE

"It's one of Springfield's major contributions to the world. Undoubtedly, it's the city's foremost contribution to the food world. Strangely, nobody's been able to explain why it isn't found in very many places outside the greater Springfield area.

"What I'm talking about is Springfield's sandwich of distinction: the Horseshoe," said Gonko.

"The men said to have created the Horseshoe at the old Leland Hotel in 1928 are Steve Tomko, retired but still living in Springfield, and Joseph Schweska, who died a number of years ago.

"The two collaborated in writing the recipe at the Leland. Tomko wouldn't give out the proportions. But even if he would, he couldn't, because he claims he never measures anything.

"The sandwich is made by laying two pieces of toast on a preheated steak sizzle platter, then placing on the toast any sort of meat, eggs, poultry, seafood or any combination of meats. Although there usually is no vegetable, a tomato or other desired vegetable can be placed on top of the first layer.

"Then comes the 'star of the show'—the creamy, slightly spicy cheese sauce. A good quantity of French fries then circles the platter, which is topped by a dash or two of paprika.

"Among the different Horseshoe sandwiches served in Springfield are ham and egg, all egg, hamburger, ham and chicken, chicken (all white meat), all ham, bacon, shrimp, turkey and corned beef.

"The sauce is the thing, as all accomplished Horseshoe chefs will tell you. Above everything else, the sharp English Cheddar cheese that Tomko and other chefs use is the basis of the sauce.

"The name *Horseshoe* was derived from the shape of the cut of ham used on the original sandwich at the Leland. Tomko and the other cooks there started with ham and then decided the sauce tasted good with every kind of meat. The French fries represent the nails of the shoe, and the sizzle platter represents a hot anvil."

During his research on the Horseshoe, Gonko found concensus among chefs that the sauce was the key. Most recommended the classic Welsh Rabbit or Rarebit sauce; others recommended a basic cream sauce with Cheddar cheese added. This sauce recipe appeared in the Christmas 1939 issue of the *Illinois State Journal*. In an article featuring favorite recipes from the chefs at the Leland Hotel, there was this recipe for Joe Schweska's version.

WELSH RAREBIT SAUCE

8 cups

¾ cup butter
¾ cup all-purpose flour
½ teaspoon salt
⅛ teaspoon cayenne
¼ teaspoon dry mustard
 1 tablespoon Worcestershire sauce
 1 quart milk, scalded
 1 pound sharp Cheddar or Old English sharp process American
      cheese, grated
 2 cups (1 pint) beer

   Melt butter in top of a double boiler over direct heat. Add flour, salt, cayenne, dry mustard and Worcestershire sauce; whisk until smooth. Cook over direct heat until bubbly. Slowly stir in scalded milk; cook until mixture thickens. Place over hot water and stir in cheese until smooth. Stir in beer just before serving.

Carol Haddix
Chicago Tribune / Chicago, Illinois

A famous Chicago treat is the hot dog. Chicago dogs are not like other city dogs, though. Here's how to make hot dogs our way.

CHICAGO HOT DOGS

1 serving

 1 Vienna frankfurter, boiled
 1 poppy seed hot dog bun
   Ballpark (prepared) mustard
   Ketchup
   Sweet pickle relish (preferably dyed bright green with food
      coloring)
   Chopped onions
   Chopped tomatoes
   Whole small hot green peppers (the hotter the better)

   Put hot dog in bun and layer each ingredient in the order given. Then try to get one end in your mouth. It's a feat to eat!

Woodene Merriman
Pittsburgh Post-Gazette / Pittsburgh, Pennsylvania

Pittsburghers have been eating the original Devonshire Sandwich, and some of its many variations, since 1934. That was the year it was "invented" in an elite supper club called The Stratford. Frank Blandi, owner of the Park Schenley restaurant now, owned The Stratford, and remembers how it happened:

"My chef, Pasquale Pirotti, was from Buffalo, New York. He made a chicken dish with a cream sauce, but it was flat." That would never do. "I'm Italian, and I don't like anything flat."

So Cheddar cheese was added to the cream sauce, some other changes were made, and the Devonshire was born. Blandi called it the Devonshire, incidentally, because of the English motif of the club. Devonshire Street was nearby.

The sandwich was an almost instant success. The restaurant had to keep making the sauce in five-gallon batches to keep up with the demand. Chefs who worked for Blandi over the years learned how to make the sandwich, taught others how to make it, and now it's served throughout the city in many variations. Crab, chicken, shrimp, tomato and asparagus often turn up in a Devonshire, depending on who's making it. But this recipe, Blandi says, is the original.

THE ORIGINAL DEVONSHIRE SANDWICH   *6 sandwiches*

6 slices toast, crust trimmed off
18 slices bacon, cooked crisp
30 thin slices cooked turkey breast
Cheese Sauce (recipe follows)
Melted butter
Grated Parmesan cheese mixed with a little paprika

For each serving, use a flat, individual-serving size, oven-proof casserole dish. Put 1 slice toast in each dish; top toast with 3 slices bacon. Add 5 slices turkey. Cover each sandwich with ⅙ of the Cheese Sauce. Drizzle with butter, then sprinkle with Parmesan cheese-paprika mixture. Bake in a preheated 450°F oven for 10 to 15 minutes, or until golden brown.

CHEESE SAUCE

5 cups

6 tablespoons butter
1 cup all-purpose flour
2 cups chicken broth
2 cups hot milk

¼ pound Cheddar cheese, grated
1 teaspoon salt

Melt butter in a large saucepan; add flour, stirring constantly. Add chicken broth and then hot milk, stirring constantly. Add cheese and salt. Bring sauce to a boil, then reduce heat and cook slowly for 20 minutes, stirring constantly. Cool to lukewarm. Beat with a wire whisk until smooth before using to make Devonshire Sandwiches.

Note: Makes enough for 6 Devonshire Sandwiches.

Christine Arpe Gang
The Commercial Appeal / Memphis, Tennessee

MEMPHIS BARBECUE

In Memphis, if a person says he wants to have a barbecue for lunch, he means a chopped barbecue pork sandwich. It is always served on a hamburger bun and is topped with cole slaw and barbecue sauce. If you don't want the slaw on the sandwich, you must always tell the person making the sandwich to hold the slaw. The pork shoulder—which barbecues slowly for 14 to 16 hours—is chopped to order as each sandwich is made. Sauces are available in hot or mild varieties. If you want mostly the interior, light, juicy meat, you ask for a white sandwich. If you like the crusty exterior, ask for it brown. If you like both, order it mixed.

Clara Eschmann
The Macon Telegraph and News / Macon, Georgia

Picnics in the deep South are always held in oak groves near a body of water to help cool the scene. Naturally, sports of all sorts are enjoyed by the guests—softball, horse shoes, swimming, races and hiding for the young children.

I've become nostalgic about this and gone back in my mind to the church picnics we had at Myrtle Springs, near my home in Americus, Georgia. The main event was when the dinner bell rang and all came to the sheltered area for the big spread of food. Following a blessing (it always seemed much too long to me as a child, because I certainly peeked at the luscious spread of food), everyone would converge upon the laden table.

A typical menu would include fried chicken, barbecue, sliced ham, homemade biscuits, deviled eggs, homemade pickles and relishes, potato salad surrounded by thick slices of vine-ripened tomatoes, pimiento-cheese sandwiches and potato chips. Caramel and chocolate layer cakes and lemon cheesecake were always there, and sometimes a Lane cake or a devil's food one, too. Pies included peach, blackberry, pecan or berries in season.

I well remember filling my plate with cakes and pies and having my mother tell me I'd have to share them with the whole family and eat some "substantial food." What a jolt!

Iced tea was served the "grown-ups," and the children had lemonade. (I'm sure, after all these years, that soft drinks have far outpaced the lemonade.)

PIMIENTO-CHEESE SANDWICHES   *12 sandwiches*

1 pound New York sharp
   cheese
1 jar (4 ounces) pimientos
   Cayenne, to taste
1 teaspoon Worcestershire
   sauce

Dash hot pepper sauce
Coarsely ground black
   pepper, to taste
Mayonnaise
24 slices bread (white or whole
   wheat)

Grate cheese on small side of a hand grater in a large mixing bowl. Drain liquid from pimientos; mash with a fork and add to cheese in bowl. Add cayenne, Worcestershire sauce, hot pepper sauce and black pepper to taste. Add enough mayonnaise (about 3 tablespoons) to reach desired consistency and mix thoroughly. Use hands or a big, wide fork to mix. Mixture will become firmer as it sets in refrigerator.

Trim edges of bread. Spread each slice of bread with mayonnaise on one side. Put cheese filling on 12 slices of bread, then put the other 12 mayonnaise-coated bread slices on top. Slice sandwiches diagonally or into strips. Be sure to put lots of filling into sandwiches.

Side Dishes

Phyllis Hanes

The Christian Science Monitor / Boston, Massachusetts

The recipe for Boston Baked Beans was submitted, naturally, by both food editors from the Boston area. Gail Perrin of The Boston Globe *noted that Vermonters insist on using maple syrup instead of molasses in their baked beans. Because these baked beans are typical of all of New England, not just Boston, we'll call them New England Baked Beans.*

NEW ENGLAND BAKED BEANS
12 servings

2 cups dried pea beans
½ pound salt pork with rind
½ teaspoon salt
1 tablespoon dark molasses

1½ tablespoons granulated
    sugar
1 teaspoon dry mustard
3 cups hot water
3 small onions

Pick over and wash beans. Cover with cold water and soak overnight in a large saucepot or Dutch oven.

In the morning, drain beans, cover with fresh water, heat slowly, and simmer until skins burst. (You can test by taking a few beans on the tip of a spoon and blowing on them. When cooked, skins will burst.) Drain.

Scald pork. Cut off a piece and put in bottom of bean pot. Slice remaining piece to the rind at ½-inch intervals, making cuts about 1-inch deep. Pour beans into pot, filling only three-fourths full, and bury pork in beans, leaving rind exposed.

Mix together salt, molasses, sugar, mustard and hot water in a bowl; pour over beans. Bury onions in top of bean pot. If beans are not completely covered with liquid, add more boiling water. Cover beanpot and bake in a 275°F oven 6 to 8 hours. Uncover during last hour to let rind get brown and crisp. Look at beans every hour or so to see if water is needed and add to keep it level with top.

Billie Bledsoe

San Antonio Express-News / San Antonio, Texas

The lowly dried bean was the cowboy's staple, so much so that mealtime often was called "bean-time." The frijole (free-holy)—kidney, red or pinto beans—will keep almost forever. No amount of cooking can really harm it, although about five hours usually does it right.

A small dish of ranch-style beans, served in their own spicy cooking liquid, was traditionally the first thing set on the table in many Texas inns. It still is, in a few.

FRIJOLES A LA CHARRA   *8 servings*

2 small ham hocks
4 cans (15 ounces each) pinto
   beans
   Juice from 1 bulb garlic, or
   to taste
⅔ teaspoon cumin seeds
1 small green pepper, finely
   chopped

2 or 3 sprigs cilantro (Chinese
   parsley), minced
1 medium onion, finely
   chopped
1 can (16 ounces) tomatoes
1 tablespoon chili powder
   Pinch salt

Cook ham hocks in a large saucepot with as little water as possible, until meat is tender. Allow hocks to cool slightly; remove meat from bones. Drain beans in colander; rinse in cold water and drain well. Put beans in saucepot with ham and cooking liquid. Add garlic juice, cumin seeds, green pepper, cilantro, onion, tomatoes with liquid, chili powder and salt. Cook over medium heat until beans are hot and flavors are blended.

Serve with cooking liquid in small pottery bowls. Old-timers say these beans taste better eaten with a spoon.

Christine Arpe Gang
The Commercial Appeal / Memphis, Tennessee

Fried Dill Pickles were made famous by the former Hollywood Cafe, which was just south of Memphis in Hollywood, Mississippi. The restaurant was best known for its pickles and frogs' legs. All of the food was mighty greasy, but people seemed to love it.

FRIED DILL PICKLES   4 to 6 servings

3 to 4 large dill pickles, whole
½ cup all-purpose flour
¼ cup beer
1 tablespoon cayenne
1 tablespoon paprika

1 tablespoon black pepper
1 teaspoon salt
2 teaspoons garlic salt
3 dashes hot pepper sauce
Vegetable oil for frying

   Cut dill pickles into slices of ¼-inch thickness. Combine flour, beer, cayenne, paprika, pepper, salt, garlic salt and hot pepper sauce in a medium mixing bowl. Dip pickle slices into batter. Heat oil to 375°F in a large, deep saucepan. Fry pickles until they float to the surface, about 4 minutes.

Mary Alice Powell
The Blade / Toledo, Ohio

This recipe is a Toledo native. It is so named because it was served for many years at the Tally Ho Restaurant. It is served as a main course side dish, even though it is sweet.

TALLY HO TOMATO PUDDING   4 servings

1 cup light brown sugar
1 cup tomato puree
¼ cup water

2 cups bread cubes, crusts
   removed
½ cup melted butter

   Combine brown sugar, tomato puree and water and cook 5 minutes. While tomato mixture is cooking, put bread cubes in a casserole and pour butter over. Add tomato mixture. Bake in a 325°F oven 50 minutes.

Woodene Merriman
Pittsburgh Post-Gazette / Pittsburgh, Pennsylvania

Exactly where Pittsburgh Potatoes originated is a mystery, but the dish is a local specialty that turns up consistently on hotel menus. Chefs tell me that it is just a recipe that was handed down from chef to chef, and that everybody knows how to make it.

PITTSBURGH POTATOES   *8 servings*

Salted water	3 pimientos, chopped
4 cups peeled and cubed potatoes	2 cups medium white sauce (see any basic cookbook)
1 medium onion, chopped	1 cup grated mild cheese

Bring a large pot of salted water to a boil. Add potatoes and onion. Cook for 5 minutes. Add pimientos and continue cooking for 7 minutes. Drain.

Turn mixture into a buttered 2-quart baking dish. Cover with white sauce and cheese. Bake in a 350°F oven 15 to 20 minutes, or until potatoes are tender.

Anne Byrn Phillips

The Atlanta Journal-Constitution / Atlanta, Georgia

Georgia's Vidalia onions are becoming more famous each year, competing with those from Maui and the Northwest. This is a delicious way to prepare Vidalias. It is excellent with steaks or roast beef.

VIDALIA ONION CUSTARD   *4 servings*

2 pounds Vidalia onions, sliced thin
3 tablespoons butter
1 cup milk
2 eggs
1 egg yolk
1 teaspoon salt
¼ teaspoon ground nutmeg
Pepper, to taste

Cook onions in butter in a large skillet over moderate heat, stirring occasionally, for 30 to 40 minutes, or until golden and soft. Let onions cool.

Whisk together milk, eggs, egg yolk, salt, nutmeg and pepper in a large bowl. Beat mixture until well combined. Stir in onions. Transfer to a well-buttered baking dish.

Bake in a 325°F oven 40 to 50 minutes, or until lightly golden and a skewer inserted in the center comes out clean. Serve hot or at room temperature.

Bernie Arnold

Nashville Banner / Nashville, Tennessee

When you say you're from the South, people just automatically think of hot biscuits and grits. I don't want to disappoint anybody, so here's one of my family's favorites.

GARLIC CHEESE GRITS   *8 servings*

½ cup grits (not instant)
2 cups water
½ teaspoon salt
½ cup butter or margarine

1 stick (6 ounces) garlic cheese
   spread, cut into chunks
1 egg
Milk

Combine grits, water and salt in a saucepan. Cook over medium heat until slightly thick. Add butter and cheese. Stir over low heat until both are melted. Break egg into a measuring cup; add enough milk to make ⅔ cup. Stir egg mixture into grits and mix well.

Pour into a greased 13x9x2-inch baking dish. Bake in a 350°F oven 20 minutes, watching carefully, or until golden brown. Allow to stand 10 to 15 minutes to thicken. Serve warm.

Louise Dodd

The Courier Herald / Dublin, Georgia

Probably any grits dish is Southern through and through, but this one is appreciated by Yankees, too. A friend served this at a meal following a concert by the World's Greatest Jazz Band; these much-traveled musicians loved it and took the recipe and bags of grits back "Nawth" with them.

CAVIAR-TOPPED BAKED GRITS   *12 or more servings*

2 cups quick-cooking grits
1 cup milk
4 eggs, beaten
1 package (3 ounces) cream
   cheese
6 tablespoons butter
1 pound bacon, cooked and
   crumbled

1 can (8 ounces) water
   chestnuts, drained and
   chopped
1 can (8 ounces) mushroom
   pieces, drained
½ cup chopped pecans
3 cans (4 ounces each) red
   caviar

Cook grits according to package directions. Add milk, eggs, cream cheese and butter; blend well. Stir in bacon, water chestnuts, mushrooms and pecans, blending well. Spoon into greased, shallow 2-quart baking dish. Bake in a 350°F oven 20 to 30 minutes. Spread caviar on top. Serve hot.

Donna Segal

The Indianapolis Star / Indianapolis, Indiana

Indiana is one of the major corn-producing states. Come July, residents have difficulty waiting until it is time to pull and cook the wonderful ears of goodness.

We love corn fixed every way, but especially roasted over a charcoal grill or gently boiled only minutes after it has been pulled.

When I was growing up, my parents were known for their large cookouts, featuring hamburgers and roasted corn. While my Dad, Gib Salle, soaked the ears, my Mom, Sarah, made the patties and put her famous green beans on to cook.

GIB'S ROASTED CORN   6 *servings*

1 dozen ears of corn in the shuck
1 bucket water
  Grill, heated until the coals are white

Pull back shucks just enough to remove silks from ears. Don't worry if all the silks can't be removed. Reclose shucks tightly around kernels. Put ears, stem-side up, vertically in bucket of water. Let corn soak at least 30 minutes. (It can soak up to two hours.)

When coals are hot, remove corn from water, shaking each ear thoroughly to remove excess water. Place ears on grill; do not stack. Thoroughly wet a large towel and tightly wring it out. Place towel over corn, so that ears are completely covered. Be sure towel covers ears and does not rest on grill.

Let corn cook on one side for 5 to 8 minutes. Remove towel and place in bucket of water to soak. Using large tongs, turn ears. The husks on the cooked side should be nicely roasted. Wring out towel and again place on ears. Cook 8 to 10 minutes, or until ears are roasted on the other side. If ears are really large, the corn may have to be turned again to ensure all sides are cooked.

Keep ears warm in a low oven if they are not to be served immediately.

To serve, pull back husks and break off stem.

Note: The ears are so good, butter and salt are not needed, although most people do add a little. I like them just the way they are.

Jalapeños are a part of Texas cooking. The addition of these hot peppers to rice gives this casserole a Texas flavor.

JALAPENO PEPPER RICE   *4 to 6 servings*

1 cup regular long-grain rice, cooked
2 cups dairy sour cream
1 can (4 ounces) jalapeño peppers, seeded and chopped
   (see note)
½ cup grated Cheddar cheese

Blend cooked rice with sour cream in a bowl; stir in jalapeños. Place mixture in a buttered 1¾- or 2-quart baking dish, or a shallow casserole dish. Top with grated cheese. Bake in a 350°F oven 20 minutes, or until heated through.

Note: Always be careful when working with hot peppers, fresh or canned, because the peppers and the fumes they release when cut can be irritating to the eyes and skin. Some cooks prefer to wear rubber gloves when handling jalapeños. Seed the peppers, then chop; or buy canned, seeded peppers. Do not put your hands near your eyes after working with peppers. Green chilies may be substituted for jalapeños for a milder taste.

When August and September come to the Sonoran Desert in Southern Arizona, it's time to gather the purple-red fruit of the prickly pear cactus and make it into jelly and other good foods. Juiced in a blender, it goes into gelatin salads or drinks. Or cut up the fruit (after carefully removing the peel and stickers, and the seeds), and use it in fruit-nut bread. Or, boil and mash the fruit, then strain the juice to make a gorgeous red jelly.

Experienced hands always use a pair of tongs to avoid the stickers when picking the ripe fruit.

USING THE FRUIT OF THE PRICKLY PEAR CACTUS

To juice: Wash the fruit in the sink, drain and transfer 7 or 8 good-sized fruit to the blender, using tongs. Slice the fruit in half with a long knife, add ¾ to 1 cup water and blend for a few seconds. Strain through cheesecloth to remove the stickers, peel and seeds. (No, the stickers absolutely will not go through the cheesecloth!)

Use the juice to flavor and color any fruit drink or punch, or use as any other juice to make gelatin dishes, being certain to add a little lemon juice to enhance the flavor.

To make jelly: Slice pears in half (without peeling) into a large kettle and add water to barely cover. Boil until tender, about 25 minutes. Press with potato masher and strain through jelly bag or two thicknesses of cheesecloth. (Stickers will not go through.) At this point, juice may be frozen for making jelly later.

To 2½ cups juice, add one 1¾-ounce package powdered fruit pectin. Bring to fast boil, stirring constantly. Add 3 tablespoons lemon or lime juice and 3½ cups granulated sugar. Bring to a hard boil. Cook for 3 minutes at a rolling boil (or until mixture sheets from a metal spoon). Remove from heat, skim off any foam, ladle into sterilized canning jars. Adjust 2-piece lids. Invert jars for a few seconds; return upright and let cool out of drafts. Test for seal. Label and store in cool, dry, dark place.

Breads

Barbara Gibbs Ostmann
St. Louis Post-Dispatch / St. Louis, Missouri

Alligator Rolls may not be originally from St. Louis, but local folks tend to think they are the creation of the Stix, Baer and Fuller Tea Room. This recipe isn't from Stix (a department store), but the resulting rolls are similar to those served there.

ALLIGATOR ROLLS
16 rolls

Rolls:
3¾ cups unbleached all-purpose flour, or more, as needed, divided
2 cups lukewarm water, divided
1 tablespoon active dry yeast
1½ teaspoons salt
Yellow cornmeal

Crunchy Topping:
2 tablespoons active dry yeast
1 cup lukewarm water
4 teaspoons granulated sugar, divided
2 tablespoons safflower or corn oil
1⅔ cups rice flour (see note)
1½ teaspoons salt

For rolls: Measure 2½ cups flour into a large mixing bowl. Make a well in center of flour and pour in ⅓ cup lukewarm water. Sprinkle yeast over water, stir to dissolve. Cover with a tea towel and let stand until yeast is foamy. Gradually add remaining 1⅔ cups water, beating in flour until well blended. Beat vigorously about 3 minutes until air bubbles form. Cover batter with tea towel and let rest 30 minutes, or as long as 8 hours.

Sprinkle salt over batter; stir in. Gradually beat in remaining 1¼ cups flour to make a stiff dough. Turn out onto lightly floured board and knead at least 10 minutes, or until smooth and pliable but still soft, adding additional flour only as needed. Form into a smooth ball, place in lightly floured bowl and sprinkle top lightly with flour. Cover with plastic wrap and a lightly dampened terry towel. Let stand at room temperature 1½ to 2 hours, or until double in bulk.

Punch down, knead briefly (about 1 minute), cover with tea towel and let rest 10 minutes. Divide into 16 equal portions, about 2 ounces each. Form into smooth balls; cover with tea towel and let rise 1 hour.

With palm of hand, flatten each ball slightly, fold in long edges as if forming a loaf, and shape into ovals; reshape into smooth balls. Arrange on a greased baking sheet that has been sprinkled with cornmeal. Cover with tea towel and let rise 45 minutes, or until almost double in size. (At this point, they're ready to bake.)

For topping: About 20 minutes before rolls are ready to bake, sprinkle yeast over water, stir in 1 teaspoon sugar and let stand until foamy. Stir in remaining 3 teaspoons sugar, oil, rice flour and salt. Beat well; set aside.

Place a shallow pan on bottom shelf of oven and preheat oven to 375°F. Just before baking, beat topping and dip each ball of dough in mixture to coat upper one-third. Place each roll, dipped-side up, on baking sheet. (Beat topping several times during process to make sure it remains well mixed.)

Pour ½ cup water into heated pan in oven. Place baking sheet of rolls on rack above pan. Bake in the preheated 375°F oven 20 minutes, or until golden, removing water pan after first 10 minutes. Transfer rolls from baking pan to wire rack. Serve warm.

Note: Don't buy sweet rice flour; it's not the baker's kind. The appropriate rice flour is available in stores selling Oriental foods, or try a natural foods store.

Janice Okun
Buffalo News / Buffalo, New York

Roast beef on "weck" is very big in Buffalo. "Weck" is short for kummel-weck—German for caraway and Buffaloese for a four-sectioned caraway-and-salt-topped bun. Kummelweck rolls are the base of the famous roast beef on weck sandwiches served in bars around Buffalo. The roast beef is sliced very thin before your eyes and piled on the roll. The sandwich is served with horseradish.

KUMMELWECK ROLLS   *16 rolls*

4½ to 5½ cups unsifted all-
    purpose flour, divided
2 tablespoons granulated
    sugar
2 teaspoons salt
1 package active dry yeast
3 tablespoons margarine,
    softened
1½ cups hot water (120°F to
    130°F)

1 egg white, at room
    temperature
Melted butter
2 teaspoons kosher or other
    coarse pure salt, or to
    taste
2 teaspoons caraway seeds, or
    to taste

Combine 1⅓ cups flour, sugar, salt and dry yeast in a large bowl. Mix thoroughly. Add margarine. Gradually add hot water, mixing as you go, then beat 2 minutes at medium speed with an electric mixer, scraping bowl occasionally. Add egg white and another cup of flour (enough to make a thick batter). Beat at high speed 2 minutes, scraping bowl occasionally.

Stir in enough additional flour to make a soft dough. Turn out onto a lightly floured board. Knead until smooth and elastic, 8 to 10 minutes. Place in greased bowl and turn to grease top. Cover and let rise in warm place until double in bulk, about 45 minutes. (Test by pushing fingers into top of dough. If indentation remains after fingers are removed, dough is ready.)

Punch down dough and turn onto floured board. Knead gently for a minute or two. Divide dough into 2-ounce pieces (a little less than ¼ cup). You should have about 16 pieces. Form pieces into balls. Let them stand, covered, on the board for 15 minutes.

Many modern rolls are shaped by machine and have a different form, but this is how to form the rolls the "correct," or old way. Swab a small amount of melted butter on top of each round. Using a ½-inch dowel (use the handle of a wooden spoon), press across middle of each round firmly, almost to the board. Then make another crease at right angles to first crease, forming 4 equal segments. Dough, where pressed in center, will now be thin enough to almost see through it.

Gently squeeze each creased roll back together with hands. Place, buttered-surface down, on greased baking sheet. Repeat with each roll. Cover rolls and let rise in warm place until double in size, about 35 minutes.

Mix coarse salt with caraway seeds (adjust amounts to suit taste). Rub through fingers to combine flavors.

Turn each risen roll face up. With a pastry brush, lightly brush top of each roll with water, then sprinkle with caraway-salt mixture.

Place pan containing ½-inch water on bottom rack of oven. (This creates steam, which will allow rolls to bloom, which means just what it sounds like: The quartered segments will spread out gently like a flower, with a rounded rather than a peaked top.) Place rolls on rack above (or put one pan beside pan of water, if necessary). Bake in a preheated 375°F oven 25 to 30 minutes. Open oven door carefully; the steam is hot.

Cool rolls on racks, then store in as dry a place as you can find. Do not store in refrigerator, or they will weep and become soggy.

Note: A good kummelweck not only lacks the peak, it should break naturally into its four divisions with plenty of topping on each.

Phyllis Hanes

The Christian Science Monitor / Boston, Massachusetts

The Parker House, established in 1855, is one of Boston's finest hotels, where many famous people, including Charles Dickens, often stayed. It is still flourishing today and is famous as the home of Parker House Rolls, considered one of the most patrician of dinner rolls.

PARKER HOUSE ROLLS

30 rolls

1 package active dry yeast
¼ cup warm water
2 cups milk
2 tablespoons granulated sugar
1 teaspoon salt

3 tablespoons butter
6½ to 7 cups sifted all-purpose
flour, divided
1 egg, well beaten
Melted butter

Dissolve yeast in warm water. Combine milk, sugar, salt and butter in a saucepan; scald, then cool to lukewarm. Stir in yeast mixture, then add 3 cups of the flour, beating very hard, until smooth and creamy. Cover with a tea towel and place in a warm spot. Let rise until light and bubbly, about 1 hour. Mix in egg and enough of remaining flour to make a kneadable dough. Knead well, cover again, and let stand in a warm place until double in size, about 1½ hours.

Roll dough to ⅓-inch thickness on a lightly floured board. Dough will spring back at first. Cut with a 3-inch round cookie cutter. Brush each circle with a little melted butter, crease center with back of a table knife to make one straight crease across the center, then fold over in half, pinching edges together. Place rolls 1 inch apart on ungreased baking sheets. Let rise again in a warm place until almost double in size, about 45 minutes. Bake in a preheated 450°F oven 12 to 15 minutes.

Donna Segal

The Indianapolis Star / Indianapolis, Indiana

In late October, when the leaves have changed to their vibrant colors and there is just a hint of a nip in the air, we take our annual trek to Southern Indiana to enjoy Brown County. After hiking around the lake, taking in the breathtaking colorama of the hills and browsing through the quaint shops, we take our place in line at the Nashville House to wait for one of my favorite dinners.

This restaurant is an Indiana tradition, and it is always busy. It is known for its pan-fried chicken, mashed potatoes, gravy and fried biscuits with homemade baked apple butter.

This recipe is adapted from one for Nashville House biscuits. The batter makes a lot. I usually use half the dough for fried biscuits and refrigerate the rest to use later for rolled and baked biscuits. When sprinkled with confectioners sugar, the fried biscuits are similar to the famous New Orleans beignets, only the dough is heavier.

HOOSIER FRIED BISCUITS
4 to 5 dozen biscuits

1 package active dry yeast
2 tablespoons warm water
2 tablespoons granulated sugar
2 cups milk
1 teaspoon salt (optional)

About 3 cups all-purpose
flour, divided
¼ cup vegetable oil
Vegetable oil for deep-frying

Dissolve yeast in warm water. Add sugar and stir thoroughly. Heat milk slightly. Put milk and yeast mixture in a large mixing bowl or bowl of an electric mixer. Stir to mix.

Stir salt, if used, into 1 cup of the flour. Gradually add flour mixture to yeast mixture, beating well. While beating, add ¼ cup oil and enough of the remaining 2 cups flour to make a soft workable dough. Beat with a dough hook or knead dough until it is smooth and elastic.

Grease a large bowl; add dough and turn to coat all sides. Cover with waxed paper and a cloth. Let rise until double in bulk.

Punch down dough. Have oil heated to hot, but not smoking. Oil should be deep enough for deep-frying. Pinch off dough, about the size of a large walnut for small biscuits, and roll lightly in palms of hands to make a round ball. Drop balls, a few at a time, into hot oil. Balls will sink to the bottom and then rise. Cook until golden brown on one side, then turn to cook other side (sometimes balls turn by themselves in oil). Cook until biscuits are golden brown. Drain on paper towels.

Serve fried biscuits with apple butter, honey, butter, jelly or a sprinkling of confectioners sugar.

Note: If desired, fry half of dough. Cover and refrigerate remaining dough. Use refrigerated dough within two to three days. For rolled biscuits, punch down dough, then roll on a flour-dusted board to about ½-inch thickness. Cut into 3-inch rounds. Place on a greased baking sheet and let come to room temperature. Bake in a 400°F oven 10 to 15 minutes.

Kitty Crider

Austin American-Statesman / Austin, Texas

History doesn't tell us just which Southern belle was responsible or what circumstances caused her to tamper with the traditional biscuit recipe and add yeast as well as baking powder or baking soda. Maybe the family's blue ribbon cooking was at stake, or perhaps she figured if Pillsbury could refrigerate a biscuit, she could do the same.

Whatever her motives, puffy golden angel or "riz" biscuits are the result of this hybrid recipe that Alabama cooks have been stirring up for some twenty-five years. (A check through a score of cookbooks, both national and regional, found angel biscuits hidden only in Alabama recipe collections.)

Alice Jarman, who served as the director of Martha White test kitchens in Nashville for twenty-seven years, first encountered angel biscuits in the late '50s. They were called Alabama biscuits then. She renamed them "riz" biscuits and printed the recipe in a Martha White flour leaflet. Somewhere along the way, either the bread or the baker was accorded the title "angel," because the flop-proof recipe goes by that name now.

Once the biscuits are cut out, they can be allowed to rise once, for about an hour, or baked immediately. Rising will give them a roll-like texture. A bonus of angel biscuits is that the dough can be kept in the refrigerator for a week and used as needed. (Allow extra rising time if the dough is cold.)

This is my family's adaptation of a recipe from the Alabama First Lady's Cook Book. And if you are wondering what a Texas gal is doing with this recipe, I was a food editor in Alabama ten years prior to moving to Austin. It wasn't until I got to Austin and found no one baking angel biscuits that I started checking into their history.

ANGEL BISCUITS
About 36 large biscuits

⅓ cup granulated sugar
5 cups sifted all-purpose flour
3 teaspoons baking powder
1 teaspoon baking soda
2 teaspoons salt

1 cup solid shortening
1 package active dry yeast
2 tablespoons warm water
1½ cups buttermilk
Melted butter

Sift sugar, flour, baking powder, baking soda and salt into a large mixing bowl. Cut in shortening. Dissolve yeast in warm water in a small bowl. Add buttermilk and yeast mixture to flour mixture. Mix well. Knead mixture, adding more flour as needed.

Roll out amount of dough needed to ½-inch thickness. Using the rim of a juice glass or a 2½-inch biscuit cutter, cut out biscuits. Place on greased cookie sheet. Let rise until double in size. Brush tops with melted butter. Bake in a 450°F oven until brown, about 10 to 15 minutes, depending upon size.

Note: Dough may be stored in refrigerator for a week or longer. Unbaked cut-out biscuits may be frozen on a cookie sheet until hard. Then store in freezer in a plastic bag, taking out as many as needed for a meal.

Jane Baker
The Phoenix Gazette / Phoenix, Arizona

As a Midwesterner transplanted to the Southwest, I'm fascinated by Mexican and native American foods. Traditionally, the Mexican foods have gotten all the attention. But now the food specialties of the Hopis and Navajos have won acclaim.

One such food is blue corn, which most often is ground into cornmeal. Blue cornmeal is coarser in consistency than yellow or white cornmeal, and recipes made with it tend to be denser. Admittedly, things made with blue cornmeal are not particularly good looking. The pale blue-gray cornmeal turns teal or lavender when mixed with water and then back to a grayish color when baked or cooked.

Most consumers aren't going to find blue cornmeal on their supermarket shelves. Even in Phoenix it is not readily available, but blue cornmeal from the Hopi Indian Community in northern Arizona usually is available at the Gentle Strength Cooperative in Tempe, a suburb of Phoenix. It's more readily available in New Mexico and can be ordered by mail from some establishments.

This corn bread recipe, which is a variation of a favorite using yellow cornmeal, is the best of the recipes I've tried with blue cornmeal.

BLUE CORN BREAD

9 squares

1½ cups blue cornmeal
¼ teaspoon salt
1 tablespoon baking powder
1 medium onion, chopped
2 eggs, beaten
1 cup dairy sour cream
½ cup butter or margarine, melted
1 to 2 cups grated Cheddar cheese (see note)
¼ cup chopped canned green chilies

Combine cornmeal, salt, baking powder and onion in a medium mixing bowl. Make a well in center of cornmeal mixture. Add eggs, sour cream, butter, cheese and chilies; mix well. Pour into a greased 9-inch square pan. Bake in a preheated 350°F oven 40 minutes, or until knife inserted in center comes out clean. Serve warm with lots of butter.

Note: I personally like lots of cheese, so I use 2 cups grated Cheddar in this recipe. The amount used may vary, depending on your own taste. Also, you may substitute 2 tablespoons chopped jalapeño peppers for the green chilies for a hotter taste.

Janet Beighle French

The Plain Dealer / Cleveland, Ohio

At our local restored village, a rough version of Johnnycake is baked in a fireplace oven there on weekends.

HALE FARM JOHNNYCAKE   *16 squares*

½ cup solid shortening
1½ cups cornmeal (regular or the finest "coarse ground")
¾ cup unsifted all-purpose flour

¾ cup granulated sugar
½ teaspoon salt
2 eggs
1¼ teaspoons baking soda
1 cup buttermilk (see note)

Melt shortening and allow to cool somewhat. Combine cornmeal, flour, sugar and salt in a large mixing bowl. Make a well in center. Add eggs and cooled shortening. Stir baking soda into buttermilk; add to mixture in bowl, scraping out all the baking soda. Mix well.

Pour batter into a greased 8-inch square pan. Bake in a preheated 350°F oven 40 minutes. Bread is done when top is lightly browned and firm and toothpick inserted in center comes out clean. Cool a few minutes in pan. To serve, split and butter.

Note: If desired, bake in a 9-inch round cast-iron skillet and cut into wedges.

To substitute for 1 cup buttermilk, you may use 2 tablespoons vinegar or lemon juice, mixed with ⅞ cup milk and allowed to stand 5 minutes.

Spider Cake is not a cake but a corn bread which originally was cooked in a cast-iron skillet or spider. It can be used in place of rice, potatoes or grits or in place of bread. Actually, it can be used in place of both. Spider Cake is delicious with ham and red-eye gravy, but even better with butter.

I have no idea of the origin of the recipe, but I grew up with it in Texas.

SPIDER CAKE

8 to 10 servings

1 tablespoon butter or margarine
1½ cups white (never yellow) cornmeal
½ cup all-purpose flour
¼ cup granulated sugar

1 heaping teaspoon baking powder
1 teaspoon salt
2 cups milk
3 eggs
1 cup heavy cream

Preheat oven to 425°F. Put butter in a heavy 9-inch iron skillet or spider, or a deep-sided 1½- or 2-quart oven-proof casserole; place on center rack of oven. The butter will melt, almost brown, while you prepare the batter.

Put cornmeal, flour, sugar, baking powder and salt in a large mixing bowl. Sifting is not necessary. Add milk and stir until almost smooth. Add eggs and stir into batter. (A whisk does it very well.)

Pull oven rack forward until you are able to pour batter into spider without removing it from oven. Next, very carefully pour cream into center of batter in the spider. You should be able to see it spread out underneath a thin layer of the batter. It will form into a custard layer.

Bake in the 425°F oven 15 to 20 minutes, then turn heat down to 350°F and bake for another 20 minutes. If the rest of the meal is not ready, turn heat down to 250°F. The spider cake will hold another 15 minutes or so if necessary.

Note: Spider cake can be served in pie-shaped wedges or can be spooned onto plates. The custard layer will really set after the first wedge is cut.

Eleanor Ostman
St. Paul Pioneer Press and Dispatch / St. Paul, Minnesota

This is a recipe Evelyn Sponberg Young made famous during the thirty-two years she was food service director at Gustavus Adolphus College, St. Peter, Minnesota. It's a recipe she learned to make from her Swedish mother, a southern Minnesota pioneer. This recipe, exceptionally delicious, is typical of Swedish rye breads that Minnesota bakers treasure.

MINNESOTA SWEDISH RYE BREAD   3 loaves

1 cup milk
1 cup water
2½ tablespoons solid
    shortening
½ cup molasses
½ cup granulated sugar
1 teaspoon salt
1 teaspoon ground anise

2 packages active dry yeast
¼ cup warm water (105°F to
    115°F)
1 tablespoon granulated sugar
2 cups rye flour
4 to 5 cups all-purpose flour
Melted butter

Scald milk. Transfer to a large mixing bowl and add water, shortening, molasses, ½ cup sugar, salt and anise. Dissolve yeast in ¼ cup warm water and 1 tablespoon sugar in a small bowl. When milk mixture is lukewarm (90°F), add yeast mixture, then rye flour; mix until smooth. Add all-purpose flour until dough is easy to handle.

Turn dough onto floured board. Knead until smooth, about 10 minutes. Place in greased bowl and turn to grease top. Cover and let rise in a warm place until double in bulk, about 1 hour.

Measure and form into three balls. Cover and let rest 15 minutes. Form into loaves and place in well-greased 9x5x3-inch loaf pans. Cover and let rise in a warm place until double in size, about 30 minutes.

Bake in a preheated 375°F oven 35 to 40 minutes. After removing from oven, brush tops with melted butter. Remove from pans and cool on racks.

To most Northerners, mangoes are exotic tropical fruits that occasionally appear in the supermarkets with large price tags. To South Floridians with mango trees in their backyards, mangoes are as common as peaches in Georgia.

Every year, mango lovers suffer from a condition called "mango madness." For example, one local mango lover insists that the fruit Eve was tempted with in the Garden of Eden was a mango, not an apple. Others say that because the mango is so messy to eat, the only way to eat it properly is standing in a bathtub wearing a raincoat.

But there is trouble in mango paradise. Some people are allergic to the sap of the tree or the slightly oily skin of the fruit. These are usually the same people who are allergic to poison ivy. If you aren't sure if you will react, wear rubber gloves and peel the fruit under running water; don't use the same knife to cut the fruit that you used to peel the mango.

MANGO NUT BREAD

1 loaf

½ cup butter or solid
    shortening
¾ cup granulated sugar
2 eggs
2 cups sifted all-purpose flour
1 teaspoon baking soda
¼ teaspoon salt
⅔ cup finely chopped raw
    mango
1 tablespoon lime juice
½ cup chopped nuts

Cream butter and sugar in a mixing bowl. Add eggs. Stir in flour, baking soda and salt. Add mango and lime juice. Mix well. Stir in nuts. Turn into a greased 9x5x3-inch loaf pan. Bake in a 375°F oven 1 hour, or until done. Do not cut bread until the next day.

Marian Burros

The New York Times / New York, New York

This cheese bread was created by Dean Kolstad, the original owner of Ms Desserts, one of the most popular food booths at Harborplace. Someone else owns the booth now, but cheese bread is still sold there. It is sold by the slice, warm, with butter.

BALTIMORE CHEESE BREAD   *12 servings*

¼ cup plus 1 teaspoon granulated sugar, divided
3 tablespoons warm water
1 package active dry yeast
2 eggs
1 cup milk
½ cup unsalted butter, melted and cooled to room temperature
1 teaspoon salt
  About 5 cups unbleached flour, divided
1 pound Svenbo, Jarlsberg or Swiss cheese, grated
1 egg, lightly beaten, for glaze

Stir 1 teaspoon sugar into warm water in a small bowl; stir in yeast and set aside until dissolved.

Lightly beat eggs in a large bowl. Mix in remaining ¼ cup sugar, milk, butter and salt. Blend in yeast mixture. Stir in 2 cups of flour to make a dough. Stir in another 1½ cups flour, turn dough onto a work surface and knead in enough of the remaining 1½ cups flour to make a soft, smooth dough. Knead dough about 15 minutes more, or until it is smooth and satiny.

Place dough in a lightly oiled bowl, turn to lightly grease top, cover with a towel and allow to rise in a warm place until double in bulk, about 1½ hours.

Thoroughly grease a 9-inch pie plate. Punch down dough and roll it into a 16-inch round. Center dough in pie pan, pressing it snugly against edges of pan and allowing excess to hang over. Mound cheese in the center and fold and pleat dough into a turban shape by gathering it into 6 or 7 equally spaced folds, stretching dough slightly as you draw each pleat over the filling. Hold ends of dough in your hand, and twist them together tightly on top. Glaze surface by brushing with lightly beaten egg. Set aside in a warm place and let rise until double in bulk, about 45 minutes.

Bake bread in center of a preheated 325°F oven 50 minutes, or until top is golden brown and bread sounds hollow when lightly tapped on the side. Cool for 15 minutes, remove from pan and let rest another 30 minutes before slicing into wedges and serving.

This is the perfect accompaniment to Conch Chowder (see page 22).

BIMINI BREAD   *4 loaves*

2 packages active dry yeast, or 2 cakes (0.6 ounce each)
  compressed yeast
½ cup warm water (110°F to 115°F for dry yeast; 95°F for
  compressed yeast)
½ cup nonfat dry milk powder
⅔ cup granulated sugar
½ cup vegetable oil
1 teaspoon salt
2 eggs
1⅓ cups warm water
7½ cups all-purpose flour, or as needed

Soften yeast in ½ cup warm water for 10 minutes. Using a large food processor, electric mixer or wooden spoon, beat yeast mixture, dry milk powder, sugar, oil, salt and eggs until smooth. Add 1⅓ cups warm water and 2 cups of the flour; beat until smooth. Add remaining flour, a little at a time, beating well after each addition. Stop adding flour when a stiff dough is formed. Without a heavy-duty mixer or food processor, you will need to work in the last of the flour with your hands.

With dough hook or by hand on a lightly floured surface, knead until dough is smooth and elastic. Place in a greased bowl and turn to grease top. Cover and let rise until double in bulk, about 2½ hours.

Punch dough down and fold over edges, pressing until air bubbles are pushed out. Divide dough into 4 pieces. Form each piece into a loaf or ball. Place in greased 8x4-inch loaf pans or 8-inch round cake pans. Cover and allow to rise until double in size, about 1 hour.

Bake in a preheated 350°F oven 40 minutes, or until nicely browned and done. Remove from pans and cool on wire racks. Freeze extra loaves for future use.

Outside of Philadelphia, putting mustard on pretzels is viewed as being just about as kinky as talking to yourself in public ... a habit not too uncommon among the local folk either, come to think of it.

PHILADELPHIA SOFT PRETZELS

16 pretzels

1 package active dry yeast
1¼ cups warm water (110°F), divided
4 to 5 cups all-purpose flour, divided

2 teaspoons salt
4 teaspoons baking soda
Coarse salt

Dissolve yeast thoroughly in ¼ cup warm water. Stir in remaining 1 cup warm water. Mix 4 cups flour and salt in large bowl. Add dissolved yeast and mix. Add enough additional flour to make a stiff dough. Knead 10 minutes, or until smooth and elastic.

Roll dough into a ball. Place in a greased bowl, turning to coat top. Cover with a towel. Let rise in a warm place until double in bulk, about 45 minutes.

Divide dough into quarters; then divide each quarter into 4 balls of dough. Take one of the balls of dough and roll it between your hands to form a coil 20 inches long and ¼ to ⅜ inch in diameter. Shape coil into a pretzel shape, pinching ends to shaped pretzel. Shape remaining dough into coils, then into pretzels.

Dissolve baking soda in 4 cups water; bring to a boil. Drop pretzels, one at a time, into boiling water and let boil 1 minute, or until pretzel floats. Remove and drain.

Place drained pretzels on buttered baking sheets. Sprinkle with coarse salt. Bake in a 475°F oven 12 minutes, or until golden brown. Place on rack to cool. Serve with mustard.

Desserts

Carol Brock
Daily News / New York, New York

Who can name the cook who created the Brownstone Front Cake? Despite its unknown provenance, this is doubtless the most "city" of all city dishes; chocolate inside and out, it looks like the slabs of brownstones that have come to characterize a romantic version of Little Old New York. With any luck, it'll be around just as long, too.

BROWNSTONE FRONT CAKE

12 to 15 slices

2 cups unsifted all-purpose flour, spooned into cup
1 teaspoon baking soda
⅛ teaspoon salt
2 squares (1 ounce each) unsweetened chocolate
1 cup boiling water
½ cup butter

1¾ cups firmly packed light brown sugar
2 eggs, well beaten
½ cup dairy sour cream
1 teaspoon vanilla extract
Chocolate Frosting (recipe follows)

Stir flour, baking soda and salt in a bowl. Set aside.

Place chocolate in another bowl; pour boiling water on top. Set aside.

Beat butter in a large mixing bowl until soft and creamy; add brown sugar gradually, continuing to beat until creamy after each addition. Add eggs and beat smooth. To this mixture, add flour mixture alternately with sour cream, beginning and ending with flour. Stir chocolate mixture to blend; fold in with vanilla.

Pour batter into a greased and floured 9x5x3-inch loaf pan. Bake in a preheated 325°F oven 50 to 60 minutes, or until done. Cool 10 minutes. Turn out on rack. Cool. Frost with Chocolate Frosting.

CHOCOLATE FROSTING

2 squares (1 ounce each) unsweetened chocolate
2 tablespoons butter, softened
½ teaspoon vanilla extract
Pinch salt

1 to 1½ cups confectioners sugar
1 egg
¼ cup milk

Melt chocolate over hot, not boiling, water.

Beat together butter, vanilla and salt in a bowl. Beat in confectioners sugar, a small amount at a time. Then beat in egg, milk and melted chocolate. Beat well until creamy.

Spoon over loaf to glaze.

Stack Cake was a traditional pioneer wedding cake that was put together right at the wedding celebration. Each guest brought a layer of cake. Applesauce made from either fresh or dried apples was spread on each layer, then the layers were stacked. The bride's popularity could be measured by the number of stacks she had and by the number of layers in each stack. It's still a popular cake in Kentucky.

KENTUCKY STACK CAKE

24 or more servings

7 to 8 cups sifted all-purpose
   flour, divided
½ cup margarine, softened
1 box (16 ounces) light brown
   sugar
1 teaspoon baking soda
1 teaspoon salt
2 teaspoons pumpkin pie
   spice, divided

1 egg
1 cup buttermilk
3 cups fresh or canned
   unsweetened applesauce
¾ cup granulated sugar, or to
   taste

Put 7 cups flour into a large bowl. Make a well in center of flour; put margarine in well. Add brown sugar, baking soda, salt and 1 teaspoon pumpkin pie spice; work into margarine with fingers. Add egg and work into margarine-sugar mixture. Gradually add buttermilk, working in flour as you go, until all buttermilk is used and a soft dough is made. Add remaining flour, if necessary.

Divide dough into 7 equal portions. Press one portion into a greased and floured 9-inch round cake pan. Bake in a 350°F oven 10 to 12 minutes. Turn layer onto a wire rack to cool. Repeat procedure for the remaining 6 portions of dough.

Combine applesauce and remaining 1 teaspoon pumpkin pie spice. Sweeten with granulated sugar. Spread applesauce between slightly warm cake layers. Do not put filling on top layer.

Cover with plastic wrap and allow cake to age for several days for best flavor.

Pat Baldridge

Morning Advocate and State-Times / Baton Rouge, Louisiana

In Mardi Gras country, King's Cake is served from January 6, Twelfth Night, the beginning of the Carnival, until Fat Tuesday, the day before Lent begins. A tiny plastic baby or dried bean or nut is baked into each cake. (It really isn't a cake at all; it's a yeast bread, decorated in Mardi Gras colors of purple, green and gold.) The person who finds the bean, baby or nut in his slice of cake is king of the Twelfth Night Ball or of the party at which the cake is served; he chooses his queen—or the other way around.

In recent years, it has become a custom for office groups to buy a King's Cake on Twelfth Night, and the person who gets the bean furnishes the cake the next week, and so on each week until Lent begins. Or in groups of friends, the bean-finder will have the next party.

NEW ORLEANS KING'S CAKE
12 to 15 servings

   2 packages active dry yeast
   2 teaspoons granulated sugar
  ½ cup lukewarm water
4½ cups all-purpose flour, divided
  ½ cup granulated sugar
   2 teaspoons salt
   1 teaspoon ground nutmeg
  ½ cup lukewarm milk
   1 teaspoon grated lemon peel
   5 egg yolks
  ½ cup butter, cut into small pieces
   2 tablespoons butter, divided
   1 dried bean or pecan half, or small (1-inch) plastic baby
   1 egg, beaten with 1 tablespoon milk
     Additional butter, for top of cake
     Sugar tinted green, yellow and purple, about 4 tablespoons of
      each color (see directions)

Sprinkle yeast and 2 teaspoons sugar over lukewarm water. Let soften. Stir, then let sit about 10 minutes, until light and bubbly. Mix 3½ cups of flour, ½ cup sugar, salt and nutmeg well. Add yeast mixture, milk and lemon peel. Work mixture together well. (An electric mixer is fine for this.) Add egg yolks and beat in well. Work in ½ cup butter and continue to beat until butter is incorporated and mixture is smooth.

Either change to a mixer dough hook, or turn dough out on floured board and knead until smooth and elastic, working in remaining 1 cup flour gradually. Dough will not be sticky when ready.

Butter a bowl with 1 tablespoon butter; put in ball of dough and turn to coat all sides. Cover with a towel, put in a draft-free place and let rise until double in bulk, about 1½ to 2 hours.

Brush baking sheet with remaining 1 tablespoon butter. Turn dough out on floured board and form into a roll about 14 or 15 inches long. (This can be done with the hands.) Put roll on prepared baking sheet and form into a ring shape, pressing ends together to seal. Push bean or baby or nut into cake from the bottom, so that it is not visible from the top. Cover with towel and put in draft-free, warm place to rise until double in size, 45 minutes to an hour.

Brush top of cake with egg-milk wash. Bake in middle of a preheated 375°F oven until brown, about 25 minutes. Slide cake onto wire rack to cool.

Butter top of cooled cake; using each color to cover a third, spread colored sugars over top of cake.

Note: Some people knead candied citron or raisins into dough. Some use a cinnamon-brown sugar filling. But the most common King's Cake is plain. Sometimes a confectioners sugar icing (white) is applied before the colored sugars are added, but most often it is not.

To tint sugar: Put a drop of desired food color into sugar (one drop for 4 tablespoons sugar) and stir until sugar is evenly colored and brightly tinted. Green, yellow and purple are the traditional colors.

Editors from opposite ends of the country sent in the recipe for Texas Sheet Cake. Where did it get its name? "Some said it was Lady Bird's recipe. Others said no, it was called Texas Sheet Cake because of its size, or because it is rich. Whatever the reason, it is well worth baking, especially in the summer when large parties abound," wrote Janice Okun of the Buffalo (New York) News. *"The cake is quite well known in Pennsylvania and Ohio, judging from reader responses to a recent request. The cake is ultra-easy to put together. You can have the whole thing frosted and ready to go in half an hour. But it also keeps well. It is a moist, heavy cake."*

This is Dotty Griffith's version, from deep in the heart of Texas.

TEXAS SHEET CAKE

Fifteen 3-inch squares

2 cups granulated sugar
2 cups all-purpose flour
½ cup margarine
½ cup solid shortening
4 tablespoons cocoa powder
1 cup water

½ cup buttermilk
2 eggs, slightly beaten
1 teaspoon baking soda
1 teaspoon vanilla extract
Icing (recipe follows)

Sift together sugar and flour in a large bowl. Combine margarine, shortening, cocoa and water in a saucepan. Bring to a rapid boil, then pour over flour-sugar mixture; stir well. Add buttermilk, eggs, baking soda and vanilla; mix well. Pour batter into a greased 15½x10½-inch baking pan (jelly roll pan). Bake in a 400°F oven 20 minutes.

Five minutes before cake is done, prepare Icing. Spread icing on cake while it is still hot and in the pan.

ICING

½ cup margarine
4 tablespoons cocoa powder
⅓ cup milk

1 box (16 ounces) confectioners sugar
1 teaspoon vanilla extract
1 cup chopped pecans

Combine margarine, cocoa and milk in a saucepan and cook over low heat until margarine is melted. Then bring to a boil, remove from heat and add confectioners sugar, vanilla and pecans. Beat well. Use to ice cake as directed.

Barbara Gibbs Ostmann
St. Louis Post-Dispatch / St. Louis, Missouri

The mighty Mississippi rolls alongside the Arch and St. Louis, and gives its name to a regional specialty: Mississippi River Mud Cake (also called Mississippi Mud Cake). This is a good one for chocoholics.

MISSISSIPPI RIVER MUD CAKE

12 average-size or 24 small servings

1 cup butter or margarine
2 cups granulated sugar
4 eggs
¼ cup cocoa powder
¾ teaspoon salt
1½ cups all-purpose flour
1 teaspoon vanilla extract
1½ cups flaked coconut
1½ cups chopped nuts
    (preferably pecans)
1 jar (9 ounces)
    marshmallow cream, or
    miniature marshmallows
    as needed

Frosting:
⅓ cup cocoa powder
½ cup butter or margarine
½ teaspoon vanilla extract
⅛ teaspoon salt
⅓ cup light cream or milk
1 box (16 ounces)
    confectioners sugar

Cream butter and sugar in a large mixing bowl. Beat in eggs, one at a time. Sift cocoa, salt and flour, then add to egg mixture. Stir in vanilla, coconut and chopped nuts.

Pour batter into a greased and floured 13x9x2-inch pan. Bake in a 350°F oven 30 to 35 minutes, or until toothpick inserted in center comes out clean. Remove from oven and, while hot, either spread with marshmallow cream or cover with miniature marshmallows and spread them after they have melted. Let cake cool, then frost with frosting.

For frosting: Beat cocoa, butter, vanilla, salt, cream and confectioners sugar in a medium mixing bowl until fluffy. Spread over marshmallow cream on cake.

Note: No baking powder or baking soda is needed in this recipe.

Barbara Durbin

The Oregonian / Portland, Oregon

Filberts—better known in Europe as hazelnuts—are strictly a product of the Northwest, in terms of U.S. production. The Oregon crop accounts for ninety-eight percent of those grown in the States, according to the Oregon Filbert Commission.

This filbert recipe, shared by a reader, Linda Dau Gray-Fellows of Hillsboro, is an old family favorite.

FILBERT CREAM CAKE

12 servings

5 eggs
½ cup butter or margarine
½ cup solid shortening
2 cups granulated sugar
1 teaspoon baking soda
1 cup buttermilk
2 cups all-purpose flour, sifted
    twice

1 can (3½ ounces) flaked
    coconut
1 cup finely chopped or ground
    filberts (using a blender
    makes this easy)
1 teaspoon vanilla extract
    Cream Cheese-Filbert Icing
    (recipe follows)
    Whole filberts, for garnish

Separate eggs. Beat egg whites in a mixing bowl until stiff. Set aside.

Cream butter and shortening in a large mixing bowl; add sugar. Add egg yolks, one at a time, beating well after each addition. Dissolve baking soda in buttermilk; add alternately with flour to creamed mixture. Beat well. Add coconut, nuts and vanilla. Fold in stiffly beaten egg whites.

Pour batter into three greased and floured 9-inch cake pans, using about 2 cups batter for each pan. Bake in a preheated 350°F oven 25 minutes. Let cool, then remove from pans; cool completely.

Prepare icing. Spread icing between cake layers and on top of cake. Garnish top of cake with whole filberts, if desired.

CREAM CHEESE-FILBERT ICING

1 package (8 ounces)
    cream cheese,
    softened
½ cup margarine
1 box (16 ounces)
    confectioners sugar

½ teaspoon almond
    extract
¼ cup finely chopped
    or ground filberts

Combine cream cheese, margarine, sugar, almond extract and filberts in a bowl; beat well. Use to ice cake, as directed.

Ginger Johnston

The Oregonian / Portland, Oregon

This recipe was shared with us more than ten years ago by a former local blueberry grower. Although there are only roughly six hundred acres of land in Oregon in blueberry production, 1983 brought in an estimated $2 million to growers.

MELT-IN-YOUR-MOUTH BLUEBERRY CAKE   9 *servings*

2 eggs, separated
1 cup granulated sugar, divided
½ cup solid shortening
¼ teaspoon salt
1 teaspoon vanilla extract

1½ cups sifted all-purpose flour, divided
1½ cups fresh or unthawed frozen blueberries
1 teaspoon baking powder
⅓ cup milk
Additional granulated sugar

Beat egg whites with ¼ cup sugar in a medium mixing bowl until mixture forms stiff, shiny peaks. Set aside.

Cream shortening in a large mixing bowl. Add salt and vanilla. Gradually add remaining ¾ cup sugar. Add egg yolks. Beat until light and creamy.

Take a small amount of flour and toss gently with blueberries so they won't settle to the bottom; set aside. Sift remaining flour with baking powder. Add to batter alternately with milk. Fold in reserved beaten egg whites and blueberries. Pour batter into a greased 8-inch square pan. Sprinkle top of batter lightly with additional sugar. Bake in a 350°F oven 50 to 60 minutes, or until cake springs back when lightly pressed in center.

Barbara Gibbs Ostmann
St. Louis Post-Dispatch / St. Louis, Missouri

Gooey Butter Coffee Cake is a St. Louis specialty that no one else seems to have heard of or enjoyed. This is difficult for generations of St. Louisans to believe. The popular cake features a rather dry base that is more than compensated for by the deliciously gooey topping. Gooey Butter Coffee Cakes are available at most local bakeries and supermarkets, but homemade from scratch is hard to beat. Here's how to make your own.

GOOEY BUTTER COFFEE CAKE
2 cakes (18 servings)

Sweet Dough:
¼ cup granulated sugar
¼ cup solid shortening
¼ teaspoon salt
1 egg
1 cake (0.6 ounce)
   compressed yeast
½ cup warm milk
2½ cups all-purpose flour
1 tablespoon vanilla extract

Gooey Butter:
2½ cups granulated sugar
1 cup butter, softened
Dash salt
1 egg
¼ cup light corn syrup
2¼ cups all-purpose flour
¼ cup water
1 tablespoon vanilla extract
Confectioners sugar

For sweet dough: Mix sugar with shortening and salt. Add egg and beat with an electric mixer for 1 minute until well blended. Dissolve yeast in warm milk. Add flour, then milk-yeast mixture and vanilla to sweet dough batter. Mix for 3 minutes with a dough hook.

Turn dough out on floured board and knead for 1 minute. Place in a lightly greased bowl, cover with a towel and set in a warm place to rise for 1 hour.

For gooey butter: Combine sugar, butter and salt. Add egg and corn syrup. Mix enough to incorporate. Add flour, water and vanilla.

To assemble: Divide dough into two pieces. Place in two well-greased 9-inch square pans. Crimp edges halfway up side of pans so gooey butter will not run out underneath. After dough is spread out, punch holes in dough with a fork (to keep dough from bubbling when baking).

Divide gooey butter into two equal parts. Spread over dough in each pan. Let cakes stand for 20 minutes. Then bake in a 375°F oven 30 minutes. Do not overbake; topping will not be gooey if cakes are baked too long.

After cakes are cool, sprinkle tops with confectioners sugar.

GOOEY BUTTER COFFEE CAKE
(Convenience Method)

12 servings

1 box pound cake mix, or a
    2-layer yellow cake mix
4 eggs, divided
½ cup butter, melted
1 package (8 ounces) cream
    cheese

1½ tablespoons vanilla extract
1 box (16 ounces)
    confectioners sugar,
    divided

Blend cake mix with 2 eggs and melted butter; pour into a 12x8x2-inch baking dish. In another bowl, combine cream cheese, remaining 2 eggs, vanilla and confectioners sugar, minus 2 tablespoons. Mix well and spread over batter in dish. Bake in a 300°F oven 15 minutes. Remove cake from oven and sprinkle reserved 2 tablespoons confectioners sugar on top. Return to oven and continue to bake 25 minutes longer. Do not overbake; topping will not be gooey if cakes are baked too long.

Note: This coffee cake is good cold, but much better warm. And yes, this one coffee cake really does require one entire box of confectioners sugar; so don't skimp.

Charlotte Hansen
The Jamestown Sun / Jamestown, North Dakota

This is a Norwegian Apple Cake that is well liked in our area.

EPLE KAKE

6 to 8 servings

1 cup butter, melted
1 box (7 ounces) zwieback, crushed
1 cup granulated sugar
4 to 6 apples, peeled and sliced

Heat butter in a skillet until it becomes a deep brown but is not burned. Mix zwieback crumbs and sugar in a bowl; add browned butter.

Place a layer of apples in a greased 9-inch casserole, then a layer of crumb mixture; repeat until casserole is filled, reserving enough of crumb mixture to cover top of casserole. Mixture should be about 3 to 4 inches deep.

Bake in a 350°F oven 1½ hours. Serve hot or cold with whipped cream or ice cream.

Janet Beighle French

The Plain Dealer / Cleveland, Ohio

Not far east of Cleveland, the Concord grape vineyards begin. They stretch across Pennsylvania and New York, and perfume the air for miles with an aroma that brings Welch's to mind. (Indeed, that company uses most of the production.)

Geneva, Ohio, has an annual Grape Festival, which features homemade grape pies and kuchens and jams and jellies, and which has certainly popularized such recipes locally.

Actual recipes are hard to nail down, however, and inevitably they require separating the pesky skins and seeds from the pulp. After several tries, we developed a kuchen which is "faster" than previous versions, and is really quite delicious.

What is kuchen? The word may mean cake in German, but in Cleveland, it tends to mean coffee cake, with or without yeast.

FASTER CONCORD GRAPE KUCHEN   *12 servings*

Puree:
1½ cups Concord grapes,
    stems removed
¼ cup granulated sugar
1 tablespoon all-purpose
    flour
¾ teaspoon lemon juice

Batter:
3 cups unsifted all-purpose
    flour, divided
1 package active dry yeast
¾ cup milk

¼ cup water
½ cup butter
½ cup granulated sugar
1 teaspoon salt
2 eggs
½ cup dairy sour cream

Streusel:
¼ cup all-purpose flour
2 tablespoons light brown
    sugar
⅛ teaspoon ground cinnamon
2 tablespoons butter

For puree: Remove grape skins by pinching each grape at end opposite stem end. Save skins. Put pulp (with seeds) in a saucepan. Carefully cook over low heat until soft. Do not boil or delicate flavor will be destroyed. Put pulp through a food mill or sieve to remove seeds.

Return grape pulp to pan. Add skins. Stir in sugar, flour and lemon juice. Cook and stir over low heat until thickened. Remove from heat. Puree thickens as it stands.

For batter: Measure 1 cup flour into a large mixer bowl. Blend in yeast. In a saucepan, combine milk, water, butter, sugar and salt. Heat to 120°F to 130°F, stirring constantly.

Pour warm mixture into flour mixture. Add eggs and sour cream. Beat with an electric mixer for 30 seconds on low speed, scraping bowl constantly. Beat 3 more minutes at high speed. Stop mixer. Gradually stir in remaining 2 cups flour.

Grease a 13x9x2-inch casserole dish. Pour in batter. Cover and let stand 20 minutes.

For streusel: Mix flour, brown sugar and cinnamon. Cut in butter until crumbly.

To assemble: Top batter with half of streusel, then the grape puree, then remaining streusel. Pierce batter with skewer here and there so that puree runs down.

Cover and let rise above a bowl of warm water, in a turned-off electric oven or microwave oven or similar draft-free place, about 45 minutes, or until double in bulk.

Preheat oven to 375°F (but remove casserole before you do!). Bake 35 minutes, or until kuchen pulls away from sides of casserole and tests done with toothpick.

Janet Beighle French

The Plain Dealer / Ceveland, Ohio

Cleveland is Kolachy country, no matter how you spell it. Kolachy is tender pastry, usually cut in wedges, and rolled up with a filling made with fruit, poppy seeds or nuts. Some Kolachy is cut in rounds and filled in the center, some is cut in rounds and folded over. Many an ethnic holiday or family celebration would be incomplete without the platter of Kolachy.

One of our best and simplest recipes hails from Lillian Kriscak, who is of Slovak descent. She calls her Kolachy "rozki" (it's cut in circles). She always makes several fillings and carries the pastries to her three daughters' homes at Christmas and Easter. We like the apricot filling best.

SLOVAK KOLACHY

80 pastries

1 pound butter, softened	1 egg, beaten
1 pound cream cheese, softened	**Filling:**
4 cups sifted all-purpose flour	12 ounces dried apricots
2 egg yolks	Water
3 tablespoons milk	3 cups granulated sugar

Combine butter, cream cheese and flour in a large mixing bowl; cut together with pastry blender until like coarse crumbs.

Beat egg yolks with fork in a small bowl; add to crumbly mixture along with milk. Work together with hands until mixed well and mixture "comes off the hands." (Dough can be frozen at this point. Thaw completely; continue.)

Divide ball of dough into 8 wedges. Cut each wedge into 10 parts. Roll each part into a round ball. Place in a large pan with waxed paper between layers. Chill until firm.

For filling: Turn apricots into saucepan and cover with water. Cook over low heat until apricots are very soft and water is mostly absorbed and evaporated. Mash with potato masher. Add sugar. Bring to boil. Cool to very cold. Makes about 3⅓ cups of filling.

Remove 10 balls of dough at a time from refrigerator. On lightly floured board, roll each one out to a 4- to 5-inch circle, of ⅛-inch thickness. Put a rounded teaspoon of apricot filling on each round and spread, leaving a border. Roll up loosely. Place seam side down on greased cookie sheet. Bend into a crescent. Brush pastries with beaten egg.

Bake in a preheated 375°F oven just until golden, about 18 minutes.

Jean Thwaite

The Atlanta Journal-Constitution / Atlanta, Georgia

Just ask anyone from Georgia where the best peaches are grown and you can be sure the answer will be an emphatic, "Georgia." Cobbler is a traditional way to use this summer fruit.

GEORGIA PEACH COBBLER

6 to 8 servings

2 cups sliced fresh peaches (or any fresh fruit)
1 cup granulated sugar
½ cup butter or margarine

¾ cup self-rising flour (see note)
¾ cup milk
Ground nutmeg

Combine fruit with sugar in a bowl; set aside. Put butter in an 11x8x2½-inch baking dish. Place in 350°F oven to melt butter. Butter should be bubbly but not brown.

Combine flour and milk; pour over melted butter in pan. Spoon fruit mixture on top. Sprinkle with nutmeg. Do not stir. Return to 350°F oven and bake 1 hour, or until cobbler is golden brown.

Note: To make your own self-rising flour, add 1 teaspoon baking powder and ¼ teaspoon salt to ¾ cup all-purpose flour.

Jane Moulton

The Plain Dealer / Cleveland, Ohio

Elephant Ears and Funnel Cakes have been popular for years in Mennonite homes in northern Ohio. They have now become part of local carnivals and county fairs.

ELEPHANT EARS
16 to 20 ears

1¼ cups milk, scalded to just below boiling (see note)
½ cup butter or margarine
1 package active dry yeast
1 teaspoon granulated sugar
¼ cup warm water (110°F to 115°F)
2½ cups all-purpose unbleached flour
1 teaspoon salt
3 eggs
¾ cup granulated sugar
¼ teaspoon ground nutmeg (optional)
3 to 4 cups additional all-purpose unbleached flour
Vegetable oil for deep-frying
Confectioners sugar or cinnamon sugar (1 cup granulated sugar with ½ teaspoon ground cinnamon)
Baked custard or vanilla ice cream (optional)

Pour milk into a mixer bowl and add butter. Cool to lukewarm (110°F to 115°F). Soften yeast and 1 teaspoon sugar in warm water for 10 minutes, or until bubbles start to form. Add yeast mixture to lukewarm milk mixture. Gradually add 2½ cups flour and salt, beating until smooth. Cover and let stand in a warm place until full of bubbles, about 30 minutes.

Beat in eggs, ¾ cup sugar and nutmeg. Add enough additional flour to make a soft dough. (Your finger will not stick to the dough when you touch it lightly, but you will think it is going to.)

Knead on lightly floured board or with dough hook of heavy-duty mixer until smooth and elastic, about 8 minutes by hand, or 4 to 5 minutes with dough hook. Cover and let rise in warm place until double in bulk, about 1½ hours.

Punch dough down; divide dough into quarters. From each quarter, make 4 or 5 pieces, each about the size of a small handball.

Heat oil for frying to 365°F in a deep-fryer or large skillet. Work with one ball of dough at a time. Pull and stretch until dough is about 10 inches long and 6 inches wide. Fry in hot fat, poking it down frequently to keep it from puffing too much. When one side is brown, turn with tongs to cook other side. Drain on paper towels. Sprinkle with confectioners sugar or cinnamon sugar.

Repeat with remaining dough. Top Elephant Ears with baked custard or vanilla ice cream, if desired.

Note: You may substitute ⅔ cup evaporated milk plus hot water to make 1¼ cups for the fresh milk.

Unfried dough can be kept tightly covered with plastic wrap in the refrigerator for 3 to 4 days. Allow to come to room temperature before stretching individual ears.

Variation: About 1 cup raisins can be kneaded into dough before shaping.

FUNNEL CAKES

8 large funnel cakes

3 eggs
½ teaspoon vanilla extract
¼ cup granulated sugar
2 cups milk
4 cups all-purpose flour
2 teaspoons baking powder
½ teaspoon salt
  Solid shortening or vegetable oil for deep-frying
  Confectioners sugar

Beat eggs and vanilla in a mixer bowl until light and fluffy. Slowly beat in sugar; beat until thick. Slowly mix in milk.

Sift together or stir well flour, baking powder and salt. Add dry ingredients gradually to egg mixture and mix well.

Heat shortening or oil to 375°F in a deep-fryer or 10-inch skillet. To make a large funnel cake, use about ½ cup batter in a funnel with a hole about ½ inch in diameter, placing your finger over the hole as you fill funnel with batter.

Release batter over center of pan and let batter flow into hot oil in a circular pattern, in rosettes or whatever shape you desire, working from the center out. You can make cakes whatever size you like. (About 9½ inches is probably as large as you can manage.)

When brown on the under side, turn and cook until other side is brown. Drain on absorbent paper. Sprinkle with confectioners sugar. Eat hot.

Janet Beighle French
The Plain Dealer / Cleveland, Ohio

Nut-filled pastries are never missing from the table during ethnic celebrations in Cleveland. This luscious version, Slovenian Icebox Potica, hails from Lillian Hlabse, a Plain Dealer *secretary who worked for the food staff for several years. On Easter, she takes it to church, along with sausage, colored eggs and fresh horseradish, for the blessing.*

SLOVENIAN ICEBOX POTICA

Six 9-inch rolls

Dough:
1 package active dry yeast
¼ cup warm water
1 teaspoon granulated sugar
4½ cups sifted Sapphire flour
    (see note)
3 tablespoons granulated
    sugar
1½ teaspoons salt
½ cup butter or margarine,
    softened
3 egg yolks, beaten
1 cup dairy sour cream

Filling:
1 cup milk

½ cup butter or margarine,
    cut in chunks
2½ pounds walnuts, ground at
    home (see note)
1 cup dairy sour cream
1½ cups granulated sugar
2 tablespoons honey
1 egg yolk, beaten
4 egg whites, beaten stiff
2 tablespoons orange zest or
    lemon zest (optional)
1½ cups golden raisins,
    plumped 10 minutes in
    hot water, then drained
    (optional)
1 egg yolk, beaten with
    1 teaspoon water

Prepare dough the day before baking.

For dough: Soften yeast in warm water. Add 1 teaspoon sugar and let stand until foamy. Sift flour with 3 tablespoons sugar and salt into a bowl. Cut in butter.

Mix egg yolks with sour cream, then add yeast mixture. Stir liquid mixture into flour mixture. Turn out on a lightly floured board and knead about 5 minutes, or until smooth.

Place in a greased bowl, turn to grease top, cover and refrigerate overnight. Next day, remove dough from refrigerator. Let stand one hour, to come to room temperature. Meanwhile, prepare filling.

For filling: In a saucepan, combine milk and butter; heat just to boiling. Remove from heat and allow to cool.

Stir together milk-butter mixture and ground nuts. Stir in sour cream, sugar, honey and egg yolk. Blend in egg whites until completely mixed in. Stir in zest, if desired.

To assemble: Divide dough into 6 parts. Roll each part to a rectangle 9 inches wide and between 14 and 18 inches long.

After each piece of dough is rolled out, spread with one-sixth of filling. Sprinkle with raisins. Roll up, starting from narrow side, and pricking top surface as you go, to prevent cracking. Do not prick top of roll.

Place in six 9x5x3-inch loaf pans that have been lined with foil and greased. Cover and let rise 1½ hours. Brush tops of rolls with egg yolk-water mixture. Bake in a preheated 325°F oven 1 hour, or until toothpick inserted comes out clean and top is golden brown. Cool in pans for 10 minutes. Then remove from pans and finish cooling on rack. Potica can be frozen.

Note: Sapphire is hard wheat bread flour, such as King Midas or Fisher's West Coast bread flour. If all-purpose flour is used, more may be needed.

Commercially ground nuts are less oily than those ground at home.

Variation: Recipe can be made in three circular rolls, baked in 10-inch tube pans, or three 15-inch rolls plus one 8-inch roll, or any combination thereof.

Ruth Gray
St. Petersburg Times / St. Petersburg, Florida

Florida's most famous dessert is a must for visitors to the Sunshine State. There are a number of recipes for it, but this one appears to be the most popular and true to the old-time Florida spirit. Use only the small yellow (when ripe) limes of the Florida Keys, and not the larger green Persian limes for a real Key Lime Pie.

Thirty minutes in the freezer will help this recipe to set. Store it in the refrigerator (not the freezer) until serving time. Lemon or calamondin juice can be substituted. Calamondins are the small, orange citrus grown on specialty trees in Florida.

KEY LIME PIE
6 or 12 servings

1 can (14 ounces) sweetened, condensed milk (not evaporated milk)	3 eggs, separated
	Salt
½ cup Key lime juice	1 (9-inch) or 2 (8-inch) pie shells, baked and cooled

Chill milk overnight in refrigerator. Place in a large mixing bowl and beat at high speed of electric mixer for several minutes. Add lime juice a few drops at a time, using a spatula to scrape mixture from the sides. Mixture will begin to thicken. Add egg yolks, one at a time, and continue to beat. Beat egg whites until stiff and fold into mixture gently. Add a few grains of salt.

Pour filling into one 9-inch pie shell or two 8-inch pie shells. Chill several hours before serving.

Toni Griffin

The Tribune / San Diego, California

San Diegans usually enjoy jicama, a root vegetable, raw for low-calorie crunching. It is also a frequently used element in salads, or as a water chestnut substitute in stir-fried dishes. Local cooking teacher Jerrie Strom bakes this unusual pie with jicama, yielding a delicious source of conversation over dessert.

JICAMA PIE
6 to 8 servings

1 jicama (½ pound), peeled and shredded (about 2 cups)
½ cup sherry
½ cup water
¾ cup plus 2 teaspoons granulated sugar, divided
6 tablespoons all-purpose flour
¼ teaspoon salt
3 egg yolks
2 cups milk, divided
1 cinnamon stick
2½ teaspoons butter, divided
1 pie shell (9 inches), baked and cooled
¼ teaspoon ground cinnamon

Combine shredded jicama, sherry and water in a small saucepan. Bring to boil; reduce heat. Cover and boil gently 45 minutes, or until most of liquid has evaporated. Drain thoroughly. Set aside.

Mix ¾ cup sugar, flour and salt in a medium saucepan. Beat egg yolks and 1 cup milk in a small bowl; stir into sugar mixture. Add remaining 1 cup milk and cinnamon stick. Stir over medium heat until mixture boils and becomes very thick. Remove and discard cinnamon stick.

Add jicama mixture to milk mixture. Cook and stir 1 or 2 minutes longer, until mixture is very thick. Stir in 1½ teaspoons butter. Remove from heat and cool slightly.

Turn mixture into prepared pie shell. Sprinkle filling lightly with ground cinnamon and remaining 2 teaspoons sugar. Cut remaining 1 teaspoon butter into small pieces; place over filling. Broil pie 3 inches from heat 3 to 4 minutes, or until butter and sugar are melted and bubbly. Watch carefully and do not let crust burn. Cool pie slightly. Serve warm or at room temperature.

Ginger Johnston
The Oregonian / Portland, Oregon

Marionberries are a special variety of blackberry grown in Oregon. They are called marionberries because extensive testing to develop the cross was done in Marion County. However, any blackberry could be substituted in this pie recipe.

MARIONBERRY PIE
6 to 8 servings

1 cup granulated sugar
3 tablespoons quick-cooking
   tapioca, uncooked
½ teaspoon ground cinnamon
¼ teaspoon lemon juice

1 quart marionberries or
   blackberries, rinsed and
   picked over
Pastry for a double-crust pie

Mix sugar, tapioca, cinnamon, lemon juice and berries in a medium mixing bowl. Pour filling into pastry-lined 9-inch pie pan. Adjust top crust; seal and flute edges. Cut slits in top. Bake in a preheated 400°F oven 10 minutes, then reduce heat to 350°F and bake 45 minutes more. Cool before serving.

Clara Eschmann
The Macon Telegraph and News / Macon, Georgia

Georgia Pecan Pie is justly famous because our state has absolutely the most delicious pecans anywhere! They are large, sweet and oily. We refrigerate and freeze the fall crop for year-round use.

GEORGIA PECAN PIE
6 to 8 servings

4 eggs
1 cup granulated sugar
1 cup dark corn syrup
½ tablespoon all-purpose flour
¼ teaspoon salt

1 teaspoon vanilla extract
¼ cup butter, melted
2 cups pecan halves
1 unbaked 9-inch pie shell

Beat eggs well. Add sugar, corn syrup, flour, salt and vanilla. Beat well. Stir in melted butter and pecans. Pour mixture into pie shell. Bake in a 300°F oven 1 hour, or until knife inserted near center comes out clean. Cool on rack.

Sue Dawson

The Columbus Dispatch / Columbus, Ohio

Ohio has been credited with a unique, two-crusted lemon pie. We had run across the recipe several times, yet we had never seen or tasted it in our many years of living in this state. Why is it called Ohio Lemon Pie? The answer was found recently in a Shaker cookbook, which traces the pie to the early Ohio Shakers. It's a different way to make lemon pie—very lemony in taste and with a delightful texture.

The pie filling has only four ingredients. Paper-thin slices of whole lemons are mixed with sugar and allowed to stand for the sugar to draw out the juice. Beaten eggs and salt are added just before baking.

OHIO LEMON PIE
6 to 8 servings

2 lemons
2 cups granulated sugar
5 eggs

¼ teaspoon salt
Pastry for a double-crust pie

Wash lemons well and cut off ends. Place lemons on a cutting board over a bowl to catch juices. With a knife, slice into paper-thin slices. (A food processor won't slice them thin enough.) Combine lemon slices and juice with sugar in a bowl and let stand at room temperature at least 2 hours or overnight. Beat eggs with salt in a small bowl and stir into lemon mixture.

Roll out half of pastry and fit into 9-inch pie pan. Roll out second half of pastry and cut slits to allow steam to escape. Pour filling into pastry-lined pan and top with second crust. Trim and flute edge.

Bake in a 425°F oven 15 minutes. Reduce heat to 350°F and bake 30 to 40 minutes more, or until pastry is golden and knife inserted in vent hole comes out clean.

Karen Marshall

St. Louis Globe-Democrat / St. Louis, Missouri

Sugar Cream Pies are as basic in Indiana, where I grew up, as beans are in Boston or chili in Texas. You can buy them frozen in the supermarkets, and almost every pie baker has a version.

According to Marge Hanley, food editor of the Indianapolis News, *old-fashioned Sugar Cream Pie is a Hoosier tradition. As the colonies grew, and pioneers moved westward, they adapted recipes brought by early English settlers. Transparent, Buttermilk and Sugar Cream Pies evolved. Sugar Cream Pie is probably a variation of English Chess Tarts.*

Early Hoosier cooks made Sugar Cream Pie by first rubbing the unbaked pastry pie crust with butter and then pouring in a mixture of cream, sugar and flour, flavored with vanilla. While the pie baked, they periodically stirred the filling with their fingers to keep the flour from settling to the bottom and coating the crust. More modern versions save the fingers and suggest shaking or stirring the filling while baking.

SUGAR CREAM PIE

6 to 8 servings

1 cup granulated sugar
½ cup all-purpose flour, minus
   1 tablespoon

1 pint heavy cream
1 unbaked 9-inch pie shell
3 tablespoons butter

Mix sugar with flour in a medium mixing bowl. Add cream and stir well. Pour into pie shell and dot with butter. Bake in a preheated 500°F oven 5 to 7 minutes. Stir ingredients in shell and bake 5 minutes longer. Stir again and reduce oven temperature to 350°F. Bake about 30 minutes longer, or until knife inserted near center comes out clean. Cool before cutting.

Nancy Pappas
The Louisville Times / Louisville, Kentucky

At Derby time, "everyone" in Louisville makes rich "Derby Pie," but a local restaurant, The Melrose Inn, has convinced the natives that it owns the name. Hence, we call it the Run for the Roses Pie, named after the Derby's major race.

RUN FOR THE ROSES PIE

8 to 10 servings

1 cup granulated sugar
½ cup all-purpose flour
½ cup butter or margarine,
   melted and slightly cooled
2 eggs, slightly beaten
2 tablespoons bourbon

1 teaspoon vanilla extract
1 cup semisweet chocolate
   morsels
1 cup chopped nuts
1 pie shell (9 or 10 inches),
   unbaked

Combine sugar, flour, butter, eggs, bourbon and vanilla in a mixer bowl; beat until well blended. Stir in chocolate morsels and nuts. Pour filling into pie shell. Bake in a preheated 325°F oven 50 to 60 minutes, or until pie is set and top cracks. Cool on rack.

Jann Malone
Richmond Times-Dispatch / Richmond, Virginia

This is a dessert that's both impressive and easy. Strawberry and chocolate ice creams are used in this particular version, but you can use whatever flavor combinations you wish. The Mile-High Pies of my wide-eyed childhood, which were served at the Pontchartrain Hotel in New Orleans, were made with vanilla and chocolate ice creams.

This New Orleans classic has been transplanted to other parts of the country, and deservedly so, by visitors to the hotel or former residents of the area.

MILE-HIGH ICE CREAM PIE
8 to 12 servings

Crust:
1⅔ cups graham cracker crumbs (about ⅓ of a 1-pound box)
¼ cup granulated sugar
⅓ cup (5⅓ tablespoons) margarine

Filling:
1 pint strawberry ice cream
1 pint chocolate ice cream

Meringue:
8 egg whites (about 1 cup), at room temperature
¼ teaspoon cream of tartar
½ teaspoon vanilla extract
½ cup granulated sugar

Chocolate Sauce:
1 cup semisweet chocolate pieces
½ cup cream, divided

Before you do anything, make space in your freezer for a really tall pie.

Prepare graham cracker crust by crushing crackers into crumbs. If you have a food processor or an electric blender, this is a snap. If you don't have either one, break crackers into small pieces and put into a plastic bag. Seal bag, then roll a rolling pin back and forth across bag until crackers become crumbs.

If you're using the food processor, add sugar to crumbs and mix well; cut margarine into chunks and process until evenly distributed in the crumbs. If you're working by hand, put crumbs into a mixing bowl and stir in sugar. Soften margarine, then cut into crumbs.

Press crumb mixture into bottom and sides of a 9-inch pie pan. Be sure to use a smooth pan; if you use one with fluted edges, you may have trouble getting the pie out.

Put crust in freezer and take out strawberry ice cream to soften a bit.

When ice cream has softened, spoon it into pie crust. Smooth and pack down with a spoon so there aren't any bubbles. Return pie to freezer until ice cream is hard, about 1 hour.

When strawberry ice cream is hard, take chocolate ice cream out of freezer to soften. Spoon chocolate ice cream on top of strawberry and pack down firmly. Return pie to freezer until ice cream is hard.

When ice cream is hard, prepare meringue. Make sure the bowl and beaters are clean, without any trace of grease. Beat egg whites with cream of tartar and vanilla until soft peaks form. Gradually add sugar, about 1 tablespoon at a time, until sugar is dissolved and egg whites are stiff and glossy. Test for stiffness by turning bowl upside down; egg whites should not slide out. If they start to slide, beat them some more.

Spread meringue over pie, making sure to spread to edges to seal ice cream inside, or else ice cream will leak when pie is placed in oven. Make decorative swirls on top with the edge of a spoon.

Broil for about 1 minute, or until meringue browns.

Freeze pie overnight, or at least for 3 to 4 hours to allow ice cream to harden.

Just before serving, prepare chocolate sauce by melting chocolate pieces with ¼ cup of cream in top of a double boiler. Add enough additional cream so sauce will pour.

Use a hot knife (run it under hot water, then wipe it off) to cut pie into serving pieces. Drizzle chocolate sauce over the top of each piece.

Elaine Corn
The Courier-Journal / Louisville, Kentucky

Transparent Pie is similar to a number of other Southern pies—it's a rich pie made with staple ingredients that every cook already has in the cupboard. It's been popular through the years in Kentucky.

TRANSPARENT PIE   *8 servings*

1¼ cups granulated sugar,
    divided
3 tablespoons all-purpose
    flour
½ cup light cream or
    half-and-half

4 egg yolks
2 tablespoons butter, melted
1 unbaked 9-inch pie shell

Mix sugar and flour in a mixing bowl. Combine cream and egg yolks; stir well. Add to sugar mixture. Add butter; mix well. Pour into pie crust. Bake in a 350°F oven 30 to 35 minutes, or until filling is brown. Remove from oven; allow pie to cool.

Janice Okun

Buffalo News / Buffalo, New York

This exceptionally good pie is popular in a Niagara Falls restaurant, John's Flaming Hearth. This is the restaurant where Nikita Khrushchev ate a meal during a visit here. Rumor has it he never paid the bill.

JOHN'S FLAMING HEARTH PUMPKIN ICE CREAM PIE

6 to 8 servings

1 quart vanilla ice cream
1 pie shell (9 inches), baked and cooled
1 cup cooked or canned pumpkin
¾ cup granulated sugar
½ teaspoon salt
¾ teaspoon pumpkin pie spice

1 cup heavy cream, whipped
Additional whipped cream, for garnish
Syrup:
½ cup light brown sugar
¼ cup dark corn syrup
¼ cup hot water
½ teaspoon vanilla extract

Spread ice cream in pie shell. (If your pie plate is not a deep one, you might want to use a little less than 1 quart of ice cream.) Place in freezer until thoroughly hardened.

Blend together pumpkin, sugar, salt and spice in a bowl. In another bowl, whip 1 cup cream until stiff; fold whipped cream into pumpkin mixture. Spoon into frozen pie shell over the ice cream. Return to freezer until ready to serve.

Before serving, cover with additional whipped cream and drizzle syrup over the top.

For syrup: Combine sugar, corn syrup and water in a small saucepan; bring to a boil and continue to boil until it starts to thicken (but don't let it get too thick). Let cool, then add vanilla. Use to top pie as directed.

Woodene Merriman

Pittsburgh Post-Gazette / Pittsburgh, Pennsylvania

Most people know, thanks to Elaine Light and the Punxsutawney, Pennsylvania, Groundhog Club, that February 2 is Groundhog Day. If the groundhog comes out of his burrow in Punxsutawney that morning and sees his shadow, there will be six more weeks of winter. No shadow means spring is here.

Elaine Light was a reporter for the Associated Press in Pittsburgh in the late 1940s. She was sent to cover the groundhog story in Punxsutawney, but fell in love with the president of the groundhog club, married, and stayed in the little town. In the years since, she has publicized "Punxsutawney Phil" (the groundhog) throughout the country; many have heard about him through her cookbook, Gourmets & Groundhogs. *She developed a groundhog cookie and a groundhog sundae—neither of which contains groundhog—that are perfect eating every February 2. In Pittsburgh, by the way, stores sometimes sell groundhog-shaped cookie cutters just before the big day. That was Elaine Light's idea, too.*

SPICY GROUNDHOGS

12 to 15 large or 36 to 48 small cookies

2 cups sifted all-purpose flour	1 cup granulated sugar
½ teaspoon salt	½ cup molasses
½ teaspoon baking soda	1 egg yolk
1 teaspoon baking powder	Granulated sugar, for rolling out
1 teaspoon ground ginger	
1 teaspoon ground cloves	1 egg, slightly beaten
1½ teaspoons ground cinnamon	Currants or raisins, for decoration
½ cup butter, softened	

Sift flour, salt, baking soda, baking powder, ginger, cloves and cinnamon into a mixing bowl. Set aside.

Cream butter and sugar in a medium mixing bowl until fluffy. Blend in molasses and egg yolk. Stir in flour mixture and mix well. Form into a ball. Wrap in plastic wrap or waxed paper. Chill for 1 hour or longer.

Roll out a small amount of dough at a time on a sugar-sprinkled board. Roll to ⅛-inch thickness. Cut out cookies with a lightly floured cutter (preferably groundhog-shaped). Place cookies on a greased baking sheet. Brush with lightly beaten egg. Decorate with currants for eyes, buttons, etc. Bake in a preheated 350°F oven 8 to 10 minutes. Cool slightly before removing from cookie sheet.

GROUNDHOG SUNDAES

6 servings

1 quart vanilla ice cream, cut in 6 slices
6 Spicy Groundhogs (see recipe)
 Chocolate sauce (your favorite)

Place slices of ice cream on individual serving plates. Place a groundhog cookie in the center of each slice. Drizzle chocolate sauce across ice cream and on plate to suggest a shadow.

Beth Tartan

Winston-Salem Journal / Winston-Salem, North Carolina

Moravians are members of a Protestant religious sect from Central Europe who settled in North Carolina in 1766. They brought to the Carolina wilderness a strong religious faith and close-knit way of life that has fostered long-standing traditions.

For more than two hundred years, Moravians in the Winston-Salem area have been baking special wafer-thin cookies for Christmas. These interesting cookies combine the seasonal spices of ginger, cinnamon and nutmeg with the flavor of molasses to achieve a delicate, tangy taste.

MORAVIAN COOKIES

3 to 6 dozen cookies

⅓ cup light molasses
¼ cup butter or margarine, softened
2 tablespoons granulated sugar
1¼ cups sifted all-purpose flour

½ teaspoon salt
½ teaspoon baking soda
¼ teaspoon ground cinnamon
¼ teaspoon ground ginger
¼ teaspoon ground cloves

Blend molasses, butter and sugar in a medium mixing bowl. Sift flour, salt, baking soda, cinnamon, ginger and cloves. Blend sifted dry ingredients into creamed mixture; mix well. Cover tightly with plastic wrap and refrigerate for at least 2 hours. (This dough may be kept refrigerated for several days.)

True Moravian cookies are paper thin. This delicious thinness is rather difficult to achieve at home by rolling the dough. If desired, form chilled dough into a roll about 2 inches in diameter; freeze, then slice paper thin with a sharp knife and bake as directed.

To roll cookies, stretch a pastry cloth over a large cutting board. Sprinkle cloth generously with flour; rub flour into cloth with hands and brush off excess. Remove about one-third of dough from refrigerator at a time, and roll out as thin as possible. Use only as much flour as necessary to keep dough from sticking to rolling pin. Cut with round, fluted-edged pastry cutter or various shaped cookie cutters.

Place cookies on a greased cookie sheet. Bake in a preheated 375°F oven 5 to 6 minutes, or until only slightly brown; be sure to check the baking cookies carefully to keep the thin cookies from burning.

Remove from oven; cool about 3 minutes. Remove cookies from pan onto cooling rack or paper towels. When cool, store in tightly covered container.

Note: The yield will vary according to whether the dough is rolled or sliced.

Barbara Gibbs Ostmann

St. Louis Post-Dispatch / St. Louis, Missouri

Growing up in the Arkansas Ozarks, I learned to appreciate "home cooking." Most of what we ate could be called Southern, but some of it was Ozark cooking.

I can remember my grandmother making potato candy—a treat to which my sisters and I looked forward. It wasn't until years later, when I attended a cooking class on Ozark foods for the newspaper, that I realized potato candy was a distinctly regional food.

GRANDMA'S POTATO CANDY

About 72 pieces

1 teaspoon vanilla extract
¼ teaspoon salt
¼ cup mashed potatoes, unseasoned

4 cups confectioners sugar
1 cup smooth peanut butter

Add vanilla and salt to mashed potatoes. Chill.

Add confectioners sugar slowly to chilled potatoes until mixture is stiff and dry. Divide mixture into 3 parts. Working with one part at a time, roll out to about a ¼-inch thickness on waxed paper (it should form a rectangle about 4″ x 12″). Spread with a thin layer of peanut butter. Roll up as for jelly roll. Repeat with remaining potato mixture and peanut butter. Chill several hours. Slice (not too thick; this is rich). Store in refrigerator.

Sandra Day

The Times-Picayune/States-Item / New Orleans, Louisiana

Pecans are abundant in Louisiana, and pecan pralines are a classic Creole candy.

PECAN PRALINES   *36 small pralines*

3 cups firmly packed light
   brown sugar
1 cup heavy cream
¼ teaspoon salt

¼ cup butter or margarine
2 teaspoons vanilla extract
2½ cups pecan halves or pieces

Combine brown sugar, cream and salt in a large, heavy saucepan. Place over moderate heat and stir until sugar dissolves. Cover pan and boil mixture for 3 minutes; remove lid and continue cooking without stirring until mixture reaches soft-ball stage, or 232°F on a candy thermometer. Remove from heat; add butter and cool to 200°F without stirring. Add vanilla and pecans; beat until thick and creamy.

Drop mixture by teaspoonfuls onto buttered waxed paper, allowing room to spread. Let stand at room temperature until firm.

Sue Dawson

The Columbus Dispatch / Columbus, Ohio

Buckeyes, from which Ohio gets its designation as the Buckeye State, are round, nut-like seeds that are dark brown with a light tan tip. These easy-to-make candies, which taste much like the popular peanut butter cups, are made to look like their namesake. They are extremely popular here at Christmastime. Although many versions exist, I like this one the best.

BUCKEYES   *About 3 pounds candy*

1 box (16 ounces)
   confectioners sugar
½ cup butter or margarine,
   softened
1 jar (18 ounces) creamy
   peanut butter

1 package (12 ounces)
   semisweet chocolate
   morsels
1 (1-inch) square paraffin
   (see note)

Combine sugar, butter and peanut butter in a large mixer bowl. Beat until mixture is well blended and begins to cling together. Roll mixture into ¾-inch balls and place balls on waxed paper.

Melt chocolate morsels and paraffin in top of a double boiler over hot water. Stick a toothpick in a peanut butter ball and dip ball in warm chocolate so that all but tip of ball is covered. Let excess chocolate drip back into pan. Place on waxed paper. Remove toothpick. Repeat until all candy has been dipped. Pinch toothpick holes closed with fingers and smooth tops. Refrigerate.

Note: The paraffin called for is household paraffin wax, as is used for sealing jelly. The paraffin makes the chocolate easier to handle and shape, and it does not affect the taste of the candy. Consumption of such a small amount is not harmful.

Jane Mengenhauser
The Journal Newspapers / Springfield, Virginia

This candy is sold along the Skyline Drive in the Shenandoah area of Virginia.

VIRGINIA APPLE CANDY   *About 32 candies*

8 medium apples	1 cup chopped nuts (walnuts
½ cup cold water, divided	or pecans)
2 cups firmly packed light	1 tablespoon fresh lemon juice
brown sugar	½ cup confectioners sugar
2 envelopes unflavored gelatin	1 tablespoon cornstarch

Peel, core and chop apples. Place apples in a saucepan and add ¼ cup water. Cook until tender; put through a food mill or a sieve. Return to saucepan and add brown sugar. Cook over low heat until thick, about 30 minutes, stirring often.

Soften unflavored gelatin in remaining ¼ cup cold water. Mix into hot apple mixture; stir until dissolved.

Chill mixture until thickened, then stir in chopped nuts and lemon juice. Pour into an 8- or 9-inch square pan to a depth of about ½ inch. Chill until firm. Cut into squares.

Combine confectioners sugar and cornstarch and sift together. Roll squares in mixture and place each square in a paper candy cup.

Janet Beighle French

The Plain Dealer / Cleveland, Ohio

Apple orchards still produce abundantly near Cleveland, offering great variety at farm markets. The Melrose, a Jonathan-Delicious cross, is available chiefly at such outlets, although it's Ohio's "official" apple.

Maple syrup is also produced in the nearby countryside, and several energetic small towns, such as Burton and Chardon, have maple syrup festivals, with the cooking down taking place on the town square, while city firemen serve pancake breakfasts in their respective firehouses.

Here is a simple recipe that combines apples and maple syrup. It had been in our files a long time before we retested it a few years ago and decided it was too good to remain hidden.

APPLES WITH MAPLE CREAM
4 servings

4 big cooking apples
1 cup maple syrup or maple-flavored syrup
½ cup water
1 tablespoon butter or margarine
1 teaspoon all-purpose flour
½ cup light cream or half-and-half
  Julienne peel of 1 lemon

Pare apples and core with an apple corer.

Combine syrup and water in a saucepan that will just accommodate apples. Boil, uncovered, for 3 minutes. Add apples. Cover. Simmer until tender, about 3 minutes. Lift apples with slotted spoon into individual dessert dishes.

Boil syrup down to ¾ cup, which takes about 2 minutes.

Melt butter in wide 2-quart pan; blend in flour. Blend in cream, then syrup. Boil, uncovered, until reduced to 1 cup, which takes about 3 minutes. Pour over apples.

Serve warm or cool, sprinkled with lemon peel.

Note: Use McIntosh, Golden Delicious, Melrose, Winesap, Jonathan, Rome Beauty or other similar apples.

Of all the recipes I've ever published, this is the one for which I've had the most requests.

PENNSYLVANIA APPLE PANCAKE   *4 servings*

3 eggs
½ cup flour (preferably quick-mixing flour)
½ cup milk
¼ teaspoon salt
8 tablespoons butter or margarine, divided
3 or 4 tart apples

3 tablespoons granulated sugar, or to taste (depending on tartness of apples)
Cinnamon-sugar (3 tablespoons granulated sugar mixed with 1 teaspoon ground cinnamon)
Lemon wedges

Preheat oven to 450°F while preparing batter. Beat eggs in a medium bowl; add flour, milk and salt and beat. Slightly lumpy batter makes a light pancake.

Melt 2 tablespoons butter in a large oven-proof skillet. Pour batter into skillet and immediately place in preheated 450°F oven; bake 15 minutes. Reduce oven temperature to 350°F and bake 10 minutes longer, or until crisp and golden.

While pancake bakes, prepare apples. Peel, core and cut apples into thin slices. Melt remaining 6 tablespoons butter in a large skillet. Sauté apples with sugar in butter 5 minutes, or less, just until crisp-tender. Set aside.

Remove baked pancake from oven. Transfer apples with slotted spoon and place over half of pancake surface. Fold pancake in half. Pour butter from skillet over pancake. Sprinkle generously with cinnamon-sugar. Cut pancake in wedges and serve with lemon.

Note: Make sure your skillet handle can tolerate 450°F heat or you'll have a souffléed handle.

Jane Baker

The Phoenix Gazette / Phoenix, Arizona

While visiting Santa Fe, New Mexico, I had this extraordinary bread pudding. Cheddar cheese adds a different twist. It is a favorite New Mexico dessert that is sometimes called sopa, which means dry soup and often refers to a dessert such as this. In New Mexico, it sometimes is called capirotada. Whatever the name, it has become a favorite of mine.

NEW MEXICO BREAD PUDDING

8 to 10 servings

1 loaf (16 ounces) white bread, sliced
1 cup raisins
1½ quarts water, divided
1 pound Cheddar cheese, shredded

2 cups firmly packed light brown sugar
3 teaspoons ground cinnamon
1 teaspoon ground nutmeg
2 tablespoons butter or margarine

Toast bread slices lightly. Remove some of the crusts, if desired. Soak raisins in 2 cups warm water until puffy. Layer bread, cheese and raisins with soaking water in a 13x9x2-inch baking dish. Start with a layer of bread and continue alternating layers until all of the bread, cheese and raisins are used. Try to end with a cheese layer.

Dissolve brown sugar, cinnamon and nutmeg in remaining 1 quart water in a large saucepan. Add butter. Bring to a boil; reduce heat and simmer for 15 minutes.

Pour hot syrup slowly over layers in baking dish until all ingredients are completely soaked. Bake, covered, in a 350°F oven 1 hour. Serve hot or chilled.

Pat Baldridge
Morning Advocate and State-Times / Baton Rouge, Louisiana

This is a classic New Orleans dessert.

BREAD PUDDING WITH WHISKEY SAUCE
6 to 8 servings

2 cups milk
4 cups day-old French bread
   cubes (½-inch pieces)
¼ cup butter, melted
½ cup granulated sugar
2 eggs, slightly beaten

¼ teaspoon salt
½ cup raisins
1 teaspoon ground cinnamon
   Whiskey Sauce (recipe
   follows)

Scald milk. Put bread cubes in a large bowl; pour milk over bread cubes. Cool. Add butter, sugar, eggs, salt, raisins and cinnamon; mix well. Pour into a greased 1½-quart casserole dish. Put casserole in a pan of hot water (1 inch deep). Bake in a 350°F oven 1 hour, or until knife inserted into pudding comes out clean. Serve warm with Whiskey Sauce.

WHISKEY SAUCE
¾ cup

½ cup butter or margarine
1 cup granulated sugar

1 egg, beaten
¼ cup whiskey

Cook butter and sugar in a double boiler until mixture is thick and sugar is dissolved. Add spoonful of mixture to egg, then stir egg into butter-sugar mixture. Cool slightly; add whiskey. Serve hot or cold over Bread Pudding.

The persimmon is to Indiana what the cranberry is to New England. The first settlers who crossed the Appalachian Mountains discovered a beautiful, amber-colored fruit tree growing wild in fields and lightly wooded areas of Ohio and Indiana—the native American persimmon.

Round to oval in shape and bright orange to almost black in color, the American persimmon is native to the entire southeastern part of the United States and grows wild over most of Southern Indiana.

Full of tannin and "puckery" when not ripe, persimmons must be left to ripen on trees before they are edible. Once they reach full color and succulent softness, they drop to the ground, ready for harvest. Some don't survive the fall, but persimmons should never be picked from trees.

Indiana settlers learned from the Indians how to add honey, cornmeal or other coarse ground meal to persimmon pulp to make simple puddings or breads. Some were cooked over the open hearth or steamed in black iron kettles. Today Hoosier cooks make everything from cakes and breads to pies, cookies, sauces, mousses and even ice cream from the legendary persimmon. Treasured persimmon puddings have become traditional Thanksgiving and Christmas desserts.

INDIANA PERSIMMON PUDDING　　　　*10 to 12 servings*

2 cups persimmon pulp
　(see note)
2 cups granulated sugar
2 eggs, beaten
1¾ cups sifted all-purpose
　flour
2 teaspoons baking powder

1 cup buttermilk
1 cup half-and-half or light
　cream
1 teaspoon baking soda
⅓ cup butter
¼ to ½ teaspoon ground
　cinnamon

Combine pulp, sugar and eggs in a large mixing bowl; mix well. Combine flour and baking powder; set aside. Combine buttermilk, half-and-half and baking soda. Add alternately with flour mixture to pulp mixture.

Meanwhile, melt butter in a 13x9x2-inch baking pan; brush to coat pan. Pour remaining butter into pulp mixture. Stir in cinnamon. Pour mixture into buttered pan. Bake in a preheated 325°F oven 55 to 60 minutes, or until set. Pudding will be dark, heavy and moist with a rather leathery, shiny top and bottom. The consistency is thicker and more dense than pumpkin pie filling. Serve warm or cold.

Note: It takes six to twelve Indiana persimmons to make 1 cup pulp. To obtain pulp: Wash persimmons well; remove and discard caps and black tips. Quarter or halve persimmons, then press through a colander. Frozen pulp is available in some stores. If using frozen pulp, thaw in refrigerator overnight and then bring to room temperature before mixing pudding.

The large Japanese or Oriental persimmons raised in California and available in supermarkets are good for salads and fresh fruit desserts. These can be put through a colander to make pulp, but they don't have the intensity of flavor best for a baked pudding. It takes only two large California persimmons to make 1 cup pulp.

Woodene Merriman

Pittsburgh Post-Gazette / Pittsburgh, Pennsylvania

To salt—or not to salt—the pecans in the Toasted Pecan Balls. That is the issue in Pittsburgh. Toasted Pecan Balls are found on many restaurant menus in the city. But some use salted chopped pecans, some prefer them plain. Either way, it's a typical Pittsburgh dessert.

TOASTED PECAN BALLS

For each serving:
1 scoop vanilla ice cream
   Chopped toasted pecans,
      salted or plain

1 (or more) topping of your
   choice: chocolate or
   butterscotch sauce,
   whipped cream, etc.

Roll round scoop of ice cream in chopped nuts until well coated. Place in dessert dish. Add topping (or toppings) of your choice.

Note: For convenience, you may want to freeze the nut-coated ice cream balls until ready to serve.

They are called CCBs, these Chocolate Crumble Balls of vanilla ice cream, rolled in crushed chocolate cookies and topped with a hot fudge sauce so thick you can eat it with a fork. The stuff of which dreams are made, they are the all-time favorite food at the Scottish Rite Dormitory at the University of Texas.

It's not often that dorm food is so good that alumnae still talk about it many years later, but CCBs are the exception to the rule. CCBs have been on the dorm menu since the 1930s; students know about them before they arrive, having been cautioned by their alumnae mothers to "watch out for the desserts." The popular dessert was included in a cookbook produced by the dorm in 1982, much to the delight of UT graduates who then were able to make the recipe at home.

CCBS (Chocolate Crumble Balls)   *8 servings*

1½ cups chocolate cookie crumbs (made from creme-filled
        sandwich-style chocolate cookies, such as Oreos or Hydrox)
1½ quarts vanilla ice cream
    Hot Fudge Sauce (recipe follows)

Crush or grind cookies (with filling) to make fine crumbs. Using a medium scoop, make 8 balls of ice cream. Roll ice cream balls immediately in crumbs, place in serving dishes and top with Hot Fudge Sauce.

If preferred, after balls have been rolled in cookie crumbs, they can be frozen on a cookie sheet until ready to serve.

HOT FUDGE SAUCE   *3 cups*

½ cup butter
1 can (5⅓ ounces) evaporated milk
2½ cups confectioners sugar, unsifted
6 squares (1 ounce each) unsweetened chocolate
1 teaspoon vanilla extract

Melt butter in a double boiler. Add evaporated milk, sugar and chocolate. Heat, stirring occasionally, until chocolate melts, about 30 minutes. Remove from heat. Add vanilla and stir vigorously.

Sauce is best when served warm or at room temperature. Sauce will keep indefinitely in refrigerator.

Note: Sauce is supposed to be thick. If you want a thinner sauce, add more milk or half-and-half. Do not add water.

Index

Drinks,
  Manhattan cocktail, 16
  mint julep, 16
Dumplings, liver
  (leberknaefly),53

E

Eggs
  Hangtown fry, 35
  Pontchartrain, 29
Elephant ears, 128
Eple Kake (Norwegian apple
  cake), 123

F

Fajitas (marinated skirt steak in
  tortillas), 63
Filbert cream cake, 120
Fish
  beer-battered, 46
  chowder, Maine, 18
  dip, smoked, 13
  Door County boil, 45
  lutefisk, 40
  salmon, grilled rice-stuffed,
    40
  soup, Chicago, 21
  stew (cioppino), 24
French dressing, 28
Frijoles a la charra (ranch-style
  beans), 89
Frosting/icing
  chocolate, 114
  cream cheese-filbert, 120
  for Mississippi River Mud
    cake, 119
  for Texas sheet cake, 118
Fry bread, Navajo, 79
Fudge sauce, hot, for CCBs,
  150
Funnel cakes, 129

G

Garlic cheese grits, 93
Georgia peach cobbler, 127
Georgia pecan pie, 133
German potato salad, 32
Gib's roasted corn, 94
Goetta (Cincinnati variation on
  scrapple), 50
Gooey butter coffee cake, 122;
  convenience method, 123
Grandma's potato candy, 141
Gravy
  cream, for chicken-fried
    steak, 61
  red-eye, for country ham, 49
Grits, 93
Groundhogs, spicy (cookies),
  139
Gumbo, chicken and sausage,
  55

H

Hale Farm johnnycake, 106
Ham
  and oyster pie, 38
  and red-eye gravy, 49
  Southern Maryland stuffed,
    47
  Tennessee country, how to
    cook, 48
Hangtown fry, 35
Hollywood Brown Derby Cobb
  salad, original, 28
Hoosier fried biscuits, 103
Hot dogs, Chicago, 83
Hot fudge sauce, for CCBs, 150
Hot tamale pie, 70
Hungarian almonds, 10

I

J

K

L

M

N

R

Ranch-style beans (frijoles a la charra), 89
Red beans and rice, 49
Rhode Island clam cakes, 39
Rice
  jalapeño pepper, 95
  red beans and, 49
  salmon, grilled rice-stuffed, 40
Rolls, 98-102
Run for the Roses pie, 135
Rye bread, Minnesota Swedish, 108

S

Salad
  Cobb, original Hollywood Brown Derby, 28
  eggs Pontchartrain, 29
  German potato, 32
  Italian, 30
  jicama, 30
  shrimp, Cumberland Island, 43
  spinach with hot bacon dressing, 31
Salmon, grilled rice-stuffed, 40
Sandwiches
  onion, 8
  original Devonshire, 84
  Louisville hot brown, 81
  Memphis barbecue, 85
  Philadelphia cheese-steak, 80
  pimiento-cheese, 86
  Springfield horseshoe, 82
Sauce
  barbecue, basic, 64
  barbecue, LBJ, 65
  cheese, for Devonshire sandwich, 85

chocolate, for mile-high ice cream pie, 136
hot fudge, for CCBs, 150
Welsh rarebit, for Springfield horseshoe, 83
whiskey, for bread pudding, 147
Sausage
  and chicken gumbo, 55
  goetta, 50
  low-country boil, 44
  red beans and rice, 79
Scrapple, 51
Sheet cake, Texas, 118
Shrimp
  Cumberland Island, 43
  De Jonghe, 41
  étouffée, 42
  low-country boil, 44
Side dishes, 88-96
Slovak kolachy, 126
Smoked fish dip, 13
Smothered burritos, 77
Soup
  bean, Spanish (potaje de garbanzos), 25
  Chicago fish, 21
  chicken booyah, 25
  conch chowder, 22
  Maine fish chowder, 18
  Minnesota wild rice, 20
  New England clam chowder, 19
  peanut, creamy, 27
Spanish bean soup (potaje de garbanzos), 25
Spicy groundhogs (cookies), 139
Spider cake (corn bread), 107
Spinach
  pizza, Chicago stuffed, 75
  salad with hot bacon dressing, 31

Springfield horsehoe (meat
    sandwich with cheese
    sauce), 82
Stack cake, Kentucky, 115
Stew
    fish and shellfish (cioppino),
        24
    ground beef (picadillo), 23
Sugar cream pie, 135
Sundaes, groundhog, 139
Swedish rye bread, Minnesota,
    108

T

Tacos, Navajo, 78
Tally Ho tomato pudding, 90
Tamale pie, hot, 70
Tennessee country ham, how to
    cook, 48
Texas cheese dip, 10
Texas chicken-fried steak, 61
Texas chuck wagon chili, 67
Texas pit barbecue, basic
    barbecue sauce for, 64

Texas sheet cake, 118
Toasted pecan balls, 149
Tomato pudding, Tally Ho, 90
Topping, for alligator rolls, 98
Transparent pie, 137
Turkey
    Louisville hot brown, 81
    original Devonshire
        sandwich, 84

V

Vidalia onion custard, 92
Virginia apple candy, 143

W

Welsh rarebit sauce, for
    Springfield horseshoe, 83
Whiskey sauce, for bread
    pudding, 147
White beans and tasso, 52
Wild rice soup, Minnesota, 20